CELTIC-MI

CELTIC-MINDED

510 Days in Paradise

JOCK BROWN

MAINSTREAM
PUBLISHING
EDINBURGH AND LONDON

First published in Great Britain in 1999 by
MAINSTREAM PUBLISHING COMPANY (EDINBURGH) LTD
7 Albany Street
Edinburgh EH1 3UG

ISBN 1 84018 226 1

A catalogue record for this book is available from the British
Library

Typeset in Berkeley Book
Printed and bound in Great Britain by Butler & Tanner Ltd

Contents

CHAPTER 1

The Initiation

'Am I speaking to the new general manager of Celtic?'

The caller on my mobile telephone was Brian Scott of the Scottish *Daily Mail*. I was in Larnaca, Cyprus, talking to a prospective new head coach who was on holiday on the island.

I was taken aback. Having reached agreement with Fergus McCann, the managing director of Celtic less than twenty-four hours earlier, I was astonished to receive such a call and to find that the news of my joining Celtic had become public.

My three weeks of discussions and negotiations had ended on the afternoon of Thursday, 19 June 1997. An agreement was reached for me to take up the brand new post of General Manager, Football, at Celtic and the extent to which this appointment was to change my life should have been apparent immediately.

I asked Fergus when he wanted me to start work, since I was scheduled to go on holiday to the United States for two weeks that weekend. His reply should have alerted me to the reality of life at a major football club.

'I need you to start immediately – I want you to be in Cyprus tomorrow to talk to a prospective new head coach.'

His response did not come in the form of a request, but more as an instruction, indeed, an expectation.

During our discussions I had been advised of the position relating to the appointment of a new head coach and I had made it clear that I thought it preferable for the head coach to be announced before the general manager. The worst situation would be that both were announced at the same time. He made it clear to me that this was not possible and whatever flak resulted from the appointments being announced the wrong way round would have to be taken.

In these circumstances I suggested that the announcement of my appointment should be made the following morning because not a whisper of the situation had been leaked until that point. The urgency of the trip to Cyprus prevented that, however, and it was agreed that an announcement would be made on the morning of Monday, 23 June.

I left for Cyprus at the crack of dawn on Friday, 20 June, to meet our candidate. Simultaneously, Fergus flew off in a totally different direction to meet another candidate. Around lunchtime on Saturday, 21 June, we were both back in Glasgow to compare notes. Only then did I discover the full extent of the research carried out by the club in its quest for the correct head coach. I also heard for the first time, in the context of coaching, the name Wim Jansen.

Unlike a very large number of football followers in Scotland, I remembered Wim from his exploits as a player for Holland in the 1974 and 1978 World Cups. I was not aware of his coaching credentials, or of his current whereabouts. Fergus explained to me that he had been recommended to him as a likely candidate for the post, having completed a contract in Japan about six months earlier. No meeting had been fixed until that point because Jansen had been in the United States on holiday but he was due to fly to Glasgow for a meeting on Monday, 23 June.

In the meantime, my non-committal response to Brian Scott's enquiry had been enough to justify him speculating on the possibility of my appointment in the Scottish *Daily Mail* on the Saturday morning. That meant relentless telephone calls from Sunday newspapermen during the Saturday, with a host of further speculative articles appearing in these newspapers the following day. I was learning for the first time the full extent of the thirst for information about any aspect of Celtic Football Club.

I spent Sunday, 22 June, at Hamilton Golf Club, where my form, surprisingly, was good. Little did I realise that I should have savoured the moment because the joys of escaping to the golf course would become rare in the months ahead.

The press conference on the Monday morning was fixed for 10 a.m. Having had a look at some of the Sunday newspapers, and having avoided daily newspaper reporters by being on the golf course, I took a conscious decision not to read any daily paper prior to the press conference announcing my appointment. This was a good decision.

I was duly smuggled into Celtic Park at 9 a.m. and met directors and senior management personnel. Peter McLean, the public relations manager with whom I was to work so closely over the following months, asked me if I had read any newspapers. He endorsed my decision and advised me that the coverage in the morning newspapers was 'mixed'. 'They are trying to make something of an alleged Rangers bias,' he told me.

Sure enough, the first question put to me at the press conference was the following: 'You will have read this morning's papers – what is your reaction?' I indicated that I had not read anything that morning and would be grateful if the journalist concerned would clarify the question. With some hesitation, he said that I had been accused in certain sections of the press of having a leaning towards Rangers and did I not think this might cause me some difficulty at Celtic?

The words 'Protestant' and 'Roman Catholic' were never used. They seldom are. At that moment I recalled the only time the issue had been raised during my discussions prior to accepting the post. I had asked Fergus McCann if he was not in any way concerned about appointing a West of Scotland Protestant to such a position within the club. 'I am not remotely interested in all that,' he had told me. He actually looked almost shocked and offended that I had raised the matter. I was delighted with both his response and his reaction.

I made it clear at the press conference that I had never in my life been either a Rangers or a Celtic supporter. For my sins, the only club which to that point generated a reaction from my heart was Hamilton Accies. I did indicate, however, that from that point on I was a huge Celtic supporter.

The fact was that during almost twenty years in the radio and television commentary box, covering countless Old Firm matches, I used to receive letters from Celtic supporters accusing me of Rangers bias and from Rangers supporters accusing me of Celtic bias. They usually arrived in approximately even numbers, and therefore I always held the view that my commentary must have been as neutral as I felt. It really was remarkable that I had never been accused of bias by a neutral football observer, only by committed followers of various clubs.

It was also abundantly clear to me that the tabloid newspapers would leave no stone unturned to establish whether I had at any time in my 51 years demonstrated an allegiance to Rangers. They would ask everyone they could find if I had ever worn Rangers colours, sung supporters' songs or generally evinced any ill will towards Celtic. I knew with complete certainty that no such evidence could ever be discovered, and that is how it turned out.

I did sense hints of hostility at that press conference. The poacher was turning gamekeeper. Perhaps it occurred to many of the journalists that if I could be appointed to such a post, so could they. And why hadn't they?

The other problem was that I was going to become privy to information which would be gold dust in the hands of a journalist. I would have the inside track on what was happening about the appointment of a head coach. I would know what transfer deals were brewing. It would be regarded by the media as intolerable if I were to keep such information to myself. It was already viewed as a serious failing that there had been no leak of my potential appointment prior to that weekend. Confidentiality had been maintained. Little did I realise the outcome of going down that path.

After the very lengthy press conference, Peter McLean showed me the *Daily Record* back-page heading: 'Joke Brown'. The paper then went on to attribute to the general secretary of the Celtic Supporters' Association comments in which he purported to express astonishment at my potential appointment because of what the Celtic supporters perceived as my Rangers bias. 'There you are,' said Peter. 'For 51 years you have been subjected to generally positive media comment and your image has not been in question. Now you have joined Celtic. You haven't done anything, you haven't made a decision, but you are now portrayed as a joke. Welcome to the club!'

Only then did the enormity of the task I was facing become apparent. I sat down to take stock of the situation. The coaching personnel had been decimated. Only Willie McStay, the head youth coach, and Danny Crainie remained. David Hay had been acting general manager and was still in place as chief scout. There was no coaching staff for the first team or for the reserve team. Pre-season training was due to start two days later. A tour to Holland had been booked for the following week, with a short tournament in Ireland to follow. It looked as though David Hay would be required to don a tracksuit to take pre-season training and this was obviously a task he did not particularly relish. In fairness to him, he had been removed from that sort of activity for some time.

I was delighted to find David at the club. I had known him for many years and had acted as his lawyer when he had his contract as manager terminated by the club in 1987. My relationship with him was excellent. It had also been made clear to me by directors that he had carried out his duties as acting general manager very effectively and diligently. I saw him as a potential major ally and someone I would be delighted to work with.

He greeted me very warmly and could not have been more helpful in these early stages. We discussed immediately the obvious difficulties presented by pre-season training starting so soon and agreed that we urgently needed to augment the coaching staff. I had been thinking about the coaching situation ever since the likelihood of my joining the club had been established. The accusation of not being 'Celtic-minded' was sure to be levelled at me constantly, and accordingly my mind had turned towards potential coaches who had Celtic backgrounds.

One of these was Murdo MacLeod. I had known Murdo for some years. I had played golf with him and had acted as his lawyer in extricating him from Dumbarton Football Club to join Partick Thistle two years earlier. After failing to have his contract renewed at Partick Thistle in May 1997, he had been in touch with me frequently to see if I could assist him in obtaining a management or coaching role at home or abroad. I put his name to Davie as potential reserve-team coach. Obviously, though, there could be no question of the appointment of a number two to the new head coach until the top man had been appointed. Davie indicated that Murdo had been in his thoughts too. He agreed to reflect on the matter overnight while I linked up with Fergus McCann to go and meet Wim Jansen. We met at One Devonshire Gardens in Glasgow.

He came over as a reserved, almost reticent man. His playing credentials were outstanding and he had clearly served his time as a coach. We were aware of the comment attributed to Johann Cruyff that Wim was one of only four men in the world who were worth talking to about football.

He was certainly intense about the game and clearly focused on the technical aspects. He had come through the Dutch School of Coaching, which was capable of rejecting such playing superstars as Johnny Rep, and he presented himself as particularly comfortable with the proposed structure within Celtic. He explained to us his time at Feyenoord and the background to his fall-outs with the head coach Wim van Hanegem and, subsequently, with the club president. It was clear that he was a very focused, single-minded man who had no interest whatsoever in the overall management of the club but only in the development of the technical side of the first team.

Interestingly, Wim explained that in his last post at Sanfrecce, Hiroshima, in Japan, he had had no capacity to bring in new players but simply had to work with the players the club provided. We made it clear to him that while there were a number of very good players at the club, we had also lost some good players and the funds were available for improving and rebuilding the side. He explained very fairly that he was a little out of touch in respect of players currently available in Europe because he had spent two years in Japan, but we clarified the fact that we had a chief scout in place who had built up a dossier of potential new recruits. It was encouraging that Wim remembered Davie Hay from the 1974 World Cup, when Davie was in Willie Ormond's Scotland squad.

The key element in Wim's discussions was dealing with the press. He made it abundantly clear that he wished to have as few dealings as possible with the media, and Fergus explained that it was the club's intention to have me as general manager fronting up communications. Accordingly, he would be spared this on a day-to-day basis. We did, however, indicate that it was imperative that he was prepared to attend pre-match and post-match interviews on an orchestrated basis. He appeared reluctant to do even that but agreed that it would be extremely difficult for him to avoid these obligations. It was also established that there would be no requirement for him to conduct any one-to-one interviews and that was a matter of immense relief to him. He appreciated that if he started doing one-to-one interviews he would have substantial difficulty rejecting others.

After that initial meeting, Wim was clearly of significant interest to us. We wondered if he might be too reserved, too introspective, and too introverted. However, technically he came with high recommendations, and he appeared to fit the brief laid down by the board for the post. He was clearly a serious candidate.

It was left that both parties should reflect on the discussions and we would contact him one way or another within a few days. As these few days elapsed, detailed consideration was given to a short list of candidates, including the two who had been spoken to the previous Friday, and Fergus consulted with other board members who required to be kept fully in the picture.

In the meantime, media interest regarding who the new head coach might be was approaching the level of hysteria. A total of thirty-three names were apparently canvassed as potentials and I was told that journalists had been put on specific bonuses to obtain the new man's identity first.

I was speaking to the press on a daily basis and could sense the growing frustration as I straight-batted all enquiries and kept insisting that we would not comment on names about whom there was speculation but would simply announce the head coach when the contract was signed. I knew this was not going down well. I made it clear that we were leaving no stone unturned to try to identify the correct man and made the point that the type of head coach we were seeking was a man who would be of interest to Real Madrid, Inter Milan, Bayern

Munich and the like. This was later used as a stick to beat me, although I stand by the comments. Had we hired Jupp Heynckes rather than Wim Jansen, the reaction of the media would, I suspect, have been similar. Yet he joined Real Madrid and won the European Cup. He was then dismissed.

Recruiting a head coach for a major football club is not like seeking a top executive for a huge industrial or commercial concern. Then, unless you know exactly who you want and proceed to headhunt him, you draw up a long leet of candidates, reduce this to a short leet after further research, enquiries and, possibly, initial interviews, and then invite the surviving candidates to attend a central venue for final interview.

This is, of course, out of the question for a big football club because of the massive media interest which afflicts not only the employer but also the prospective employee. It is obviously essential for club officials to talk to prospective head coaches, but if that fact reaches the media, the reports normally indicate that the man has been offered the post.

Similarly, if a coach who has talked to officials of a club is approached by the media, who have found out about a meeting, he is hardly likely to say, 'Yes, I've spoken to the club, but they intend to speak to other candidates, and I'm not sure I'm the man they want.' He will prefer, not unnaturally, to convey either expressly or by implication that he has been offered the job. Top coaches do not submit applications, nor do they offer themselves for interview. They want to be headhunted. They can relax, obviously, in the safe and certain knowledge that no club is going to say, 'Yes, we were thinking of Joe Bloggs, and interviewed him. But we were distinctly unimpressed and we're moving on to consider other candidates.'

The sensitivity of the whole situation is enormous. How can you be comfortable with a new head coach until you've met him? If you meet him, and you're not comfortable, you're hardly going to shaft him, nor are you keen to respond to any public utterances he makes implying the job was his for the taking.

Meanwhile, on the morning of Tuesday, 24 June, I discussed again with Davie Hay the coaching situation and the handling of pre-season training. We agreed to make contact with Murdo MacLeod and offer him the post of reserve-team coach with immediate responsibility for the pre-season training due to start on Wednesday, 25 June.

We met Murdo in the offices of Harper Macleod, the solicitors with whom I had been working until my abrupt move to Celtic. Davie and I sold the job to him. I made it clear that the only post we could offer him was reserve-team coach, and while I appreciated that this might seem a long way down from being manager of Partick Thistle both in the Premier Division and in the First Division, it brought him back to Celtic Park and put him in pole position for being selected as assistant head coach in the event that the new head coach wanted Scottish back-up.

At the same time I made it clear that in recognition of his ambitions to operate at a higher level I did not propose to put him on a fixed-term contract, which would mean that he could move to any other club as manager without compensation being required. He would simply be on a contract of employment.

Murdo agreed to accept but expressed unhappiness with the salary on offer. I should have read the signs. Nevertheless, he duly signed his contract and commenced work the following morning, taking charge of pre-season training. John Clark, the highly respected Lisbon Lion, had already been appointed kit controller before my arrival and I was delighted to find him there, since I had known him for a long time and liked and respected him.

I recall being party to a press photograph with Davie, Murdo and John in which I unashamedly played the 'Celtic connection' card. I made it clear to the press at that time that my interest was in obtaining the best people for jobs available, but if they had a Celtic background as well then that would be deemed a bonus.

At the same time, while I had made it clear to Davie Hay that I was delighted to find him at the club and looked forward to working with him, I was very sensitive to the fact that he had been acting general manager and would have been clearly disappointed at not being given the post permanently. Following discussions with the directors, the proposal arose that he should be appointed assistant general manager in addition to chief scout. The principal purpose of this appointment was to make a tangible gesture towards Davie to make him feel wanted. I was delighted to put the proposal to him and he appeared delighted to accept. It was a gesture of goodwill which was to backfire.

When pre-season training started there were two notable absentees, Paolo Di Canio and Jorge Cadete, which was wonderful fodder for the voracious media.

But the big priority remained the appointment of the head coach. Consultations and discussions among board members continued relentlessly. Speculation in the media grew to fever pitch. I fended off all enquiries in daily dealings with the press. Their frustration was obviously heightening. Journalists appeared under immense pressure.

Accordingly, as a man who they believed could relieve that pressure, I was not popular. In fact, I was not in a position to relieve the pressure because no decision had been reached. In any event, it would be a board decision, not my decision. The aspect which upset me during the thirteen days between starting work at Celtic and the appointment of a new head coach was that the delay was being portrayed as my fault. Yet the board had conducted extensive enquiries before my arrival, and had come up with a list of candidates who met the criteria they, not I, had established. I simply fell into the process on the board's terms, as was, of course, perfectly proper. The selection boiled down to Wim Jansen and two others.

A name constantly in the frame as far as the media were concerned was Bobby Robson. Indeed, when I walked into Hamilton Golf Club the following Sunday morning for a brief respite from the relentless activity at Celtic Park, I was greeted with amusement in the clubhouse by members reading the *Sunday Mail* which told them that at that very moment I was in Spain sweet-talking Bobby into coming to Celtic! The truth is that I never at any time spoke to Bobby Robson about coming to Celtic. The only time I recall speaking to him at all was when I interviewed him for television several years ago.

After that weekend the decision was taken – Wim Jansen was the man.

CHAPTER 2

Upstairs, Downstairs

It was recognised in the club that the appointment of Wim Jansen would not be heralded as a major coup by the media and thus by the supporters. But, following the departure of Tommy Burns as manager, the board had considered very carefully indeed their approach to the new structure and to the identification of the people to occupy the key posts of head coach and general manager. It is fair to say that the board was disenchanted with what they considered to be the old historical football culture. It bred an 'upstairs, downstairs' mentality which drove a wedge between directors, management, administration and technical staff.

The culture of promoting good players into managers was not deemed to be necessarily the most appropriate and successful way to go forward into the new millennium. The word 'manager' came under scrutiny and was questioned with regard to its accuracy. What top footballer has any background in 'management'? It had always occurred to me that the range and the scope of the tasks imposed on Tommy Burns were far too great for a man of his background and training.

Let me declare a position on Tommy. I like him enormously, respect him very much as a coach and wish him nothing but the good fortune he deserves in his career. Had I been appointed as general manager with Tommy as head coach I would have been delighted. I am sure we could have worked well together. Yet to ask him to undertake all the responsibilities of managing the football operation of a club like Celtic was, in my opinion, totally unfair. To fathom that reasoning, consider the job description handed to me at the time of my appointment:

JOB DESCRIPTION

Title: General Manager – Football Operations
Division: Football
Reports To: Managing Director
Direct Reports: Head Coach
                  Chief Scout
                  Manager of Youth Development
                  Physiotherapist
                  Kit Manager
                  Reserve-Team Coach

Job Function:
1   Overall responsibility for Club's football activities in all respects – performance, personnel, budgetary, staffing, within objectives approved by the Board. Accountable to the Managing Director for meeting job objectives as to team success and overall financial budgets.

2   Supervision and direction of:
• Head Coach, who has responsibility for the on-field performance of the first-team squad
• Chief Scout
• Manager of Youth Development, who covers all youth recruitment, training, and operations of a training centre Health and Fitness Department, led by Physiotherapist
• Player personnel and administrative/support group
• Kit Manager
• Reserve-Team Coach

PRINCIPAL TASKS: (*In addition to these functions, staff are required to carry out such other duties as may reasonably be required.*)

Description of Duties:
• Produces a plan for long-term development of the football division, detailing the structure, systems and procedures to be utilised and including 1–3-year projections that incorporate costs and capital expenditures.
• Responsible for achieving plan.
• Participates fully as a senior member of the corporate management team, reporting to the Managing Director.

Supervises, directs and develops the football division support staff.

- Responsible for preparing, with assistance of the Financial Director, and meeting the football operations budget, including salaries, transfer fees and other operating costs and capital expenditure.
- Negotiates contracts of employment with all support staff including a bonus scheme. Supervises and develops such members of staff, agreeing targets and objectives and undertaking annual appraisal.
- Negotiates contracts with players and agents, and administers their implementation.
- Deals with all player personnel issues, through agents or directly.
- Deals with the implementation of rules, fixture and discipline (overall scheme) matters or any direct football playing matter governed by the football authorities.
- Arranges pre-season tours, training camps, friendly and testimonial matches for the benefit of the football division and the Company as a whole.
- In conjunction with the ongoing requirements of the Head Coach, assisted by the scouting network, initiates, conducts and concludes transfer transactions to and from the Club (when appropriate, along with the Managing Director, legal adviser or other director).
- Represents the Club's football operation to the media and speaks for the Club on all football-related matters. Attends pre- and post-match press conferences along with the Head Coach.
- Attends all senior management meetings of the Club. When appropriate, attends Board meetings of the Company when invited by the Managing Director in order to provide progress reports.
- Ensures that appropriate administration procedures are in place to achieve smooth running of the Football Department's activities.
- Attends home and away matches and official functions at which representation from the Club is required. Fulfils requirements on the Club's behalf that relate to its obligation to sponsors, supporters and advertisers, and to the promotion of its products and services.
- Disciplinary procedures and plans introduced and implemented.

While, admittedly, in his role as a traditional football manager Tommy Burns would not have been required to carry out *all* the tasks on that job description, he was expected to carry out a large number of them and at the same time coach and prepare the first team for matches. If ever there was a better argument for splitting the job then I can't think what it is. It is surely imperative for the man with the technical skill to devote himself one hundred per cent to team affairs, especially at a major club like Celtic.

There are other aspects of the football culture which cause concern. Such is the uncertainty of the traditional manager's position that he tends to spend a substantial percentage of his time covering his back and trying to survive. That helps to explain why so many managers appoint trusted friends to their back-up staff and frequently take them with them when they move. The most important attribute such a back-up man can provide the number one is unswerving loyalty and trust. Whether or not he is the best man for the job can take second place. There is also the old-pals' network between players who become managers and the media. If you reflect on the number of managers with poor records who continue to obtain new posts, consider how media-friendly they are. Similarly, managers can be hounded out by an unfriendly press who will continue to make it very difficult for them to be re-employed.

Everyone in the game would have backed Roy Aitken to be an outstanding manager. The same applied to Willie Miller. However, when results started to go wrong for Willie, the fact that he was not 'user-friendly' to the media helped to bury him. Roy Aitken, who was a very popular figure among the sports journalists in Scotland as a player, became seriously disenchanted by what he thought was very unfair treatment while he was manager of Aberdeen and his relationship with the media foundered. The tragedy for both men is that they are probably more capable now of being outstanding managers than they were at the time they were in their posts, but the chances of them being welcomed back, certainly by the media, are not good.

It is also where I came to grief at Celtic. I had clear instructions to attempt to plug the information leaks from within the club and to conduct club affairs in a businesslike, professional and confidential manner. As a trained lawyer, such instructions were welcome and expected. Not commenting on speculation is natural for me but anathema to many sections of the media. So when I made it clear that the first indication of the identity of the new head coach would be at the moment he was officially announced, I could see the hackles rise. However, it is surely the correct way to operate.

Further, it seems to me that talking about a player who is registered with another club is discourteous, inappropriate and capable of being classed as tapping. I once asked journalists at a press conference what was wrong with our policy of not commenting on players registered with other clubs. The response was that there was nothing wrong with it from the club's point of view but it certainly did not suit them!

I sympathise with many of the journalists. They are under immense pressure to come up with 'exclusives'. It appears not to be enough to cover the game diligently and accurately. Sensational headlines are essential and the tag 'exclusive' must be paraded at every opportunity.

The one certain way for a journalist to provide an exclusive is to invent the story. That, I fear, is something which does occur as a result of the current pressure on journalists. The trouble is, the public swallows most of it. Accordingly, there is a serious problem which I think applies to the whole of the United Kingdom.

It relates to the power of the press to attack viciously and relentlessly when it suits them, effectively destroying people's lives or, on other occasions, building them up ready for the fall. What is clear is that people from abroad are aghast at how some sections of the press operate in this country. Some of the foreign players arriving at Celtic could not believe the coverage to which they and their colleagues were frequently subjected.

So Wim Jansen presented a problem. While the club was convinced he was the correct man for the job, we knew his arrival would not be greeted with mass outpourings of joy from the supporters because of the way in which the appointment would be portrayed by the media. Fergus McCann constantly repeated his policy: 'Do the correct thing and then deal with the public relations fall-out separately.' The alternative, of course, is to do the wrong thing because it will generate a good public reaction.

It was believed to be the correct thing to appoint Wim Jansen. But we knew there would be a public relations fall-out. The clamour among supporters is always for 'sexy' appointments or 'sexy' signings. They are told by the media to demand 'big names', both as coaches and as players. Sadly, a 'big name' is frequently someone with an impressive past but not necessarily a big future. The history of the game is littered with clubs rueing the day they spent fortunes on such big-name players. The aim of scouting should be to identify outstanding players on their way up, not after they have become household names.

Similarly with coaching, history tends to dictate that many top men have questionable playing pedigrees. Had Celtic appointed Marcello

Lippi, Ottmar Hitzfeld or Guus Hiddink instead of Tommy Burns in 1994, they would have been ridiculed. Who were they? Who had they played for? How many caps did they have? How many medals had they earned as players? What was Lippi's background before Juventus? What was Hitzfeld's track record? What were Hiddink's credentials? I'll wager that a very small percentage of Scots could have given you the answers. Yet Lippi was hugely successful at Juventus, Hitzfeld at Borussia Dortmund and Bayern Munich, and Hiddink went on to coach Holland, then Real Madrid. None was a world-renowned player.

Even within Britain, the evidence suggests that top coaches were not necessarily top players. The best Scottish-born football manager since the war, in my estimation, is Alex Ferguson. The reason? He massively improved East Stirlingshire, he transformed St Mirren, he made Aberdeen the top Scottish club over a period of eight years and he has enjoyed unparalleled success at the top level with Manchester United. Yet even Fergie would admit that his playing credentials fell far short of the likes of Denis Law and George Best. I am sure they weren't dancing in the streets of Paisley, Aberdeen and Manchester when Fergie was appointed. Massive credit is due to the respective boards for identifying his talent.

Celtic's greatest manager, Jock Stein, would certainly not claim to have been an outstanding player. Similarly, I do not remember Arsène Wenger making a huge impact on the playing side of things. When he first arrived at Arsenal from Japan, I remember the wiseacre comments ridiculing the appointment.

So an attempt was made to package Wim Jansen by the use of an endorsement from Johann Cruyff. This was designed to be window-dressing, because the board and I were confident that we were making a good appointment.

The press conference was called for 3.30 p.m. on Thursday, 3 July 1997. The media were in a frenzy. On the morning of the announcement no one had a clue who the new man would be. Unforgivable. Thus when Fergus McCann, Wim Jansen and I walked into the press conference, no one had a clue who the new man was and scarcely anyone recognised him. Unforgivable. Hence the headline in *The Sun*: 'The second worst thing to hit Hiroshima'. Welcome to Scotland, Wim.

During the discussions leading to Wim's appointment he had made it clear that he would prefer to have a Scottish number two to bring him up to speed quickly with the Scottish game. Davie Hay and I discussed the matter in some detail and decided that Wim should be given a couple of options. One was obviously Murdo MacLeod. We also identified another.

I had arranged for the second candidate to meet Wim on the evening of Thursday, 3 July, to be interviewed and to establish if the appropriate rapport existed. A highly respected Scotsman, he arrived for our meeting and indicated immediately that he proposed to disqualify himself as a candidate now that he had been made aware of the identity of the new head coach. He said to Wim, 'I presume it will be your intention to take the training on a day-to-day basis, hands on?'

Wim acknowledged that this would be the case, and in these circumstances Mr X graciously declined being considered for the post because he believed that his coaching career had gone beyond what some people term a 'bibs and cones' man to a coach who called the shots in training the first team on a day-to-day basis. He indicated that he would be frustrated if he were reduced to a secondary role while Wim took charge on the training ground.

The two men hit it off extremely well and it was a matter of immense regret to me that the partnership could not be put in place. Mr X has my total admiration and respect for his honesty and integrity, but how I wish he had come to Celtic.

Candidate number two, Murdo MacLeod, was already in Holland. The team had flown there early on Thursday morning to begin their pre-season preparations. The following morning, Friday, 4 July, Wim and I flew out to join them. Davie Hay was in overall charge, with Murdo in charge of training. I then made what I consider to be one of the biggest mistakes I made during my time at Celtic. I left Wim, Davie and Murdo in Holland while I came straight back to Glasgow to continue with the many other duties imposed on me by my job description. I should have remained in Holland for the week. That way I might, just might, have been able to deal better with the problems which lay ahead involving what I consider to be the collusive sub-group, the clique, of Messrs Jansen, MacLeod and Hay.

But the problems created by Messrs Di Canio and Cadete were such that I felt I had to be back in Glasgow.

CHAPTER 3

The Trading of Di Canio

Paolo Di Canio had failed to return for pre-season training on 25 June. After a number of attempts to make contact with him, a fax arrived from his agent indicating that he was unwell and not fit to return to Glasgow for training. I immediately requested a medical certificate to that effect and one eventually arrived, in Italian, confirming that he was unwell and indicating that he would arrive early the following week.

He did duly arrive, in the company of his personal trainer. Now if one thing is not required for players at Celtic it is a personal trainer. The club had acquired the services of a top-class conditioning instructor in Jim Hendry and he had made a marvellous impact on individual players by setting up programmes comprising gymnasium work and other methods of improving players' strength, suppleness and endurance. In fairness to Di Canio, however, he took his own conditioning work very seriously indeed and kept himself in immaculate shape. That was borne out by Jim Hendry after Di Canio arrived in Glasgow. The next information I received from the training staff was that Paolo would not go to Holland with the rest of the squad since he believed his fitness programme would be better served by staying in Glasgow.

The result was my only one-to-one discussion with him in my time at Celtic. I had actually spoken to him once before while conducting an interview for the BBC after one of his excellent performances for Celtic the previous season. Accordingly, the opening part of our meeting really represented something of an introduction.

I must confess that I was supremely confident that with gentle, tactful handling and the use of logic and common sense, Paolo would soon realise that it was imperative that he join the rest of the squad in Holland. I was wrong. He made it perfectly clear to me that he had no intention of going to Holland and it immediately occurred to me that he had another agenda to pursue. My contribution to the meeting became more forthright. I asked him if he thought it would be perfectly in order for Tommy Boyd to decide to train at Strathclyde Park, Alan Stubbs to select Troon Beach and Jackie McNamara Portobello. He failed to answer.

I then touched his Achilles' heel. He always prided himself on being the supreme professional, so when I suggested to him that it was totally unprofessional for him to opt out of the training camp set up for the entire squad, it had the effect of lighting the touch paper for Di Canio to explode. He simply could not tolerate being called unprofessional. The trouble was, Paolo's interpretation of 'professional' appears to differ from everyone else's. Yes, it is extremely important to keep your condition and to be as fit as possible. But it is also important to operate in the best interests of the team, to control a potentially violent temper and to consider the harmony of the squad. On these counts he failed.

The meeting broke up in disarray since he had lost his temper over the accusation of being unprofessional and I made it clear to him that it would be deemed a breach of contract if he failed to train precisely where the club instructed. My hope remained that he might see sense, relent and join the party going to Holland, but this did not happen. The players departed on Thursday, 3 July, without him, although by that time I was much more preoccupied in finalising the arrangements relating to the appointment of Wim Jansen.

The principal priority, therefore, on my return to Glasgow on the Friday evening after travelling with Wim to Holland was to deal with the Di Canio issue. I had left word in Glasgow that a meeting should take place on the morning of Saturday, 5 July, with Paolo to deal with the question of his breach of contract.

Paolo duly arrived at the appointed hour on the Saturday morning, but in the presence of his solicitor. His solicitor did all the talking and, indeed, Paolo waited outside the boardroom where the meeting involving the solicitor, the club's financial director Eric Riley and me took place. It was clear that Paolo was adamant about not travelling to Holland and I made it perfectly clear to the solicitor that the impression I had was that Paolo was operating his own agenda in the aftermath of his comments about his 'little problem' with Fergus McCann at the end of the previous season. I told the solicitor that if Paolo was trying to work his ticket to the English Premiership then there would be no co-operation from Celtic and he would have to turn his mind to implementing his contract.

The solicitor, in fairness, was in substantial difficulty because Paolo had clearly told him precisely how he wanted the matter to progress and the solicitor knew perfectly well that he was being asked to sanction a blatant breach of contract. The only note of comfort which the solicitor could provide was that Paolo had indicated that he would travel to Ireland the following week for the Umbro pre-season tournament. I remember suggesting to the solicitor, with heavy sarcasm which did me no credit, that this was very good of Paolo and wondering if he would deign to turn up for league matches as they fell due. It was an unsatisfactory meeting which ended with the imposition of disciplinary action by way of a fine on the player and with a totally uncertain future.

Could I have handled these meetings better? Maybe. But I don't think we were dealing from a straight pack of cards. It was my clear impression that there was a hidden agenda.

To be perfectly fair to Paolo, he worked his socks off in training while the players were in Holland and he did turn up at the airport the following Monday morning to travel to Ireland, but nothing was ever straightforward. He was the only player who failed to obey the dress code for travelling, a matter which caused me great concern but did not seem to trouble Wim Jansen. By that time, too, another decision had been taken. Wim had made it clear after his week in Holland that he wanted to appoint Murdo MacLeod as his number two. Believe it or not, I was delighted when Murdo gave his first interviews in that capacity at Glasgow Airport on the morning of the trip to Ireland.

I had agreed with Murdo that we would sort out the details of an adjusted contract on his return but, regrettably, that was not the only contract issue causing difficulty within the backroom staff. I still did not realise that what I now describe as the collusive sub-group involving Wim, Davie and Murdo had been formed in Holland. I was still not remotely aware of it when the trio set off for Ireland, with me staying behind once again to continue the pursuit of new players and to attempt to carry out the necessary reorganisation behind the scenes at Celtic Park. By this time Wim had identified two players he wanted to bring to the club, Henrik Larsson of Feyenoord and Regi Blinker of Sheffield Wednesday. Davie Hay had also provided a list of potential recruits to Wim, including Darren Jackson of Hibernian, Craig Burley of Chelsea and Stephane Mahe of Rennes. Final decisions would be taken immediately after Wim had seen the team in action in the tournament in Ireland.

What everyone saw in Ireland, however, was the end of Paolo Di Canio as a Celtic player. His 'little problem' had re-emerged. This apparently related to some kind of promise in Paolo's mind made by

Fergus McCann that he would be entitled to a better contract if he performed well in his first season at Celtic. Paolo clearly believed that he had, buoyed up, no doubt, by being elected Scotland's Player of the Year. Fergus McCann has always stated that no such commitment was given and I have no hesitation in believing that. However, at the same time, I wonder if someone else indicated to Paolo that his contract could be renegotiated after an impressive first season. That is simply a theory on my part and I should make it clear that I do not include as a possible purveyor of such news anyone employed by Celtic.

Whatever the background, Paolo had definitely taken umbrage towards Fergus and he certainly did not relish the disciplinary action being taken against him in terms of fines. My own further theory is that he decided then that this was the time to make his move for the English Premiership. He came back from Ireland and headed straight off to Rome indicating that he would not play for Celtic again.

As if starting a brand new career at Celtic was not difficult enough, any hopes of a gentle breaking-in period had long gone and now I was faced with a major problem in resolving the difficulties created by the temperamental Italian.

Wim Jansen was quite clear: he wanted Paolo in the team whatever it took. On one occasion, indeed, he indicated to me that he was quite sure the problem was all about money and I should simply go out to Italy and give him a new deal to bring him back. I resisted that by talking about potential dressing-room implications, a factor which I thought would have been much more in Wim's domain. I felt that we were facing a very difficult situation in that if Paolo were to be tempted back by additional money, what possible control could the club have over other players? The message, behave intolerably and earn yourself a better contract, was a dangerous one and could not be contemplated.

My view was that the best chance we had of getting Paolo back playing for Celtic was to send out the strongest possible message that he would not be transferred. The press interest in the whole issue was relentless to the point of obsession. No contact with any member of the media was possible without references to Di Canio. The message I attempted to convey through them to Paolo was that we would not be pressured into selling him but were prepared to have a stand-off in the interests of leaving him with no option but to return to Celtic to continue his career.

However, after some time it became apparent to me that Paolo's return could have serious repercussions in the dressing-room. I sensed that he had lost the respect of the other players, who were embarking on a very tough season attempting to stop a record-breaking ten championships in a row by Rangers, and it was perfectly reasonable for these players to be disenchanted with the antics of Paolo at such a time.

At that point, I started introducing to the comments I made about Di Canio the fact that while he was not for sale, *the situation would remain constantly under review*. That line seldom made any tabloid newspaper reports, if ever.

The other relevant factor was that my attempts to obtain Regi Blinker from Sheffield Wednesday had been thwarted by David Pleat, who was then in charge at Hillsborough. He had suddenly introduced to our various conversations, however, the fact that he wanted Di Canio and would only consider allowing Blinker to come to Celtic if we would allow Di Canio to go to Sheffield Wednesday. Initially I was adamant to David that Di Canio was not available.

David Pleat is a wily old fox for whom I have enormous respect. I think he was well aware that Di Canio was attempting to play in the Premiership and he also knew that he represented dead money to Celtic while he sat in Rome and contributed nothing to our team. We had many a pleasant conversation on the telephone, with me trying to winkle out Blinker, and David using the Dutchman as bait for Di Canio.

My initial impression, in any event, was that Di Canio would not be interested in going to Sheffield. The view had been formed in my mind, rightly or wrongly, that he fancied a glamour move to London. Whether or not he had been fed any encouragement via his agents in that respect I will never know, but when he embarked on his campaign to leave Celtic, I really don't think that Sheffield Wednesday, with all due respect, was what he had in mind.

Wim Jansen effectively played no part in the whole process. He showed no interest whatsoever. He simply wanted Di Canio in his team and he also wanted Blinker. Eventually I indicated to him that it was possible to have Blinker in the team but not Di Canio, and he simply retorted that he wanted both! I explained to him that Sheffield Wednesday would only release Blinker if I would involve Di Canio in the deal. Wim simply kept repeating that he wanted both of them.

By the end of July/beginning of August it was clear to me that Di Canio could not return to the dressing-room at Celtic. Wim was desperate for a naturally left-sided attacking player and the time had come, I believed, to investigate the Sheffield Wednesday position as far as finance was concerned.

Fergus McCann and the executive directors were fully aware of all the activity and were very anxious indeed to have either Di Canio in the team or an appropriate injection of capital to invest in replacement players. The possibility of precisely the situation which emerged with Pierre Van Hooijdonk at Nottingham Forest was facing Celtic, but the wild card factor was Regi Blinker. The conclusion was reached that if Di Canio was to continue the impasse by remaining in Rome, we should not allow that situation to result in the possibility of acquiring Blinker being sacrificed. My comment about the Di Canio situation being constantly under review was used more frequently and more forcibly. Once again, the reference to 'under review' scarcely saw the light of day.

Another conversation between David Pleat and me took place on the morning of Friday, 1 August, and after some lengthy haggling a deal was struck in principle, subject to both players co-operating. It was agreed that all the relevant parties should meet in Amsterdam the following day to establish if deals could be done. I still privately doubted whether or not Di Canio would agree to a move to Sheffield Wednesday. I hoped, however, that the impasse for the best part of a month would have had him twitching about his career.

That Friday I faxed Di Canio's agent and indicated to him that he was now permitted to speak to Sheffield Wednesday about a move there, but to no other club. It was imperative that it was made absolutely clear to him that if he would not entertain the Sheffield Wednesday deal, no other deal would be contemplated. Regi Blinker was the man who made the difference.

The parties all convened in Amsterdam the following morning – except Di Canio. The Sheffield Wednesday chairman, Dave Richards, made it clear that no deal could be concluded without the presence of the player. His agents indicated that he would arrive later. He didn't.

In the meantime, I agreed terms, in principle, with Regi and his agent, although he was aware that it was all entirely subject to Di Canio's co-operation. Regi and I became interested onlookers while Sheffield Wednesday tried to negotiate terms with Di Canio's agents. Eventually, having imposed a final deadline, Dave Richards succeeded in achieving an agreement, again in principle, and all subject to Di Canio's attendance and approval. It was made clear to me that the entire deal was off unless Di Canio presented himself to the Sheffield Wednesday people on satisfactory terms and concluded agreements. By the Monday evening he had still not appeared in Sheffield, apparently despite promises to the contrary. In the meantime, Regi

Blinker was in Glasgow going through his medical and sitting in a hotel awaiting Paolo's pleasure.

A press conference was due to take place at 2.30 p.m. on the Tuesday and Di Canio would obviously be the main topic once again. Half an hour before that press conference was due to start I spoke to David Pleat and he indicated to me that as far as he was concerned the deal was off. Both he and his chairman were totally disenchanted with the whole situation and were prepared to wait no longer for Di Canio's arrival. David made it clear to me that he was washing his hands of the whole affair and it was now up to his chairman whether or not he kept the door open for Di Canio.

On the basis of that information I conducted the press conference at 2.30 p.m. I should have cancelled that conference. I was bombarded with questions about Di Canio, every one of which I answered honestly on the basis of the information available at the time. Unfortunately, the lawyer in me could not resist the verbal fencing. I should have walked out after five minutes saying next to nothing. However, I indulged in the verbal sparring and was able to survive, as I saw it, by virtue of the fact that two key questions which I could not have answered adequately were never asked. I was foolish enough to tell the press that the following day, which made them love me even more!

What were the questions?

1. Have you given permission to Paolo or his agent to speak to any other club?
2. Have you agreed terms, even conditionally, with any other club?

At that conference, I kept on repeating that the Di Canio situation was constantly under review. I was so persistent that one journalist asked me if the matter was being reviewed daily, or even hourly. I confirmed that it was.

At 9 p.m. I received a call from David Pleat to the effect that Di Canio had arrived and his chairman wished to proceed with the deal. What I had agreed with Sheffield Wednesday was that in order for me to sign Regi Blinker, all that was required was for Di Canio to arrive in Sheffield to talk to them about signing. If they were not able to persuade him to sign, then I could still proceed to sign Blinker at an agreed price and Di Canio would remain a Celtic player. First thing on the Wednesday morning we arranged the press conference to announce the signing of Regi Blinker, and just before the conference started I heard from Sheffield that they had agreed terms with Di Canio.

The Blinker signing conference was largely a waste of time as far as poor Regi was concerned because the real interest on the part of the press was in the Di Canio position. Remarkable hostility was generated towards me because of the conference the previous day and no one appeared interested in the fact that the goalposts had been moved markedly the previous evening. It was put to me that I had continually said that Di Canio was not for sale and yet I had now sold him. I replied that I *had* said that but I had also said that the situation would remain under constant review, daily and even hourly. In any event, he had been 'traded', not sold, in that his departure to Sheffield Wednesday was essential to enable us to bring in a player Wim Jansen was keen to have in the team.

Peter McLean, our public relations manager, had been told by two friendly journalists about a week earlier that certain elements of the press were not happy with me and would 'slaughter' me at the first available opportunity. Apparently they were still furious about the fact that Wim Jansen had been presented without advance knowledge and that I would not co-operate by discussing players about whom there was transfer speculation. After the Blinker conference, Peter and I knew that these elements of the press were about to seize their opportunity. A huddle took place. After a press conference is concluded, many of the journalists, but not all, go into a huddle to decide how they will present the material they have obtained. Whatever then appears the next morning appears largely across the board and if a spin or twist is put on the material by one, the same spin or twist is employed by all those in the huddle.

The decision was clearly taken here to 'slaughter' Brown. So forget all about the Di Canio situation being under daily or even hourly review, forget all about the changing circumstances between Tuesday afternoon and Tuesday evening. The opportunity of teaching me, and Celtic, a lesson was apparently too good to miss.

En masse, the huddle members portrayed me as a liar and as someone who had deliberately deceived them over Di Canio. This was patently inaccurate. But what every editor would have read in most competing papers matched, so they would come to the conclusion that their own reporters had handled the matter accurately. You see, none of the editors or newspaper executives appears to want to accept that his or her reporter is party to the huddle process. That's what gives each huddle member his safety net. I must emphasise that not every football journalist joins the huddle, nor operates in this manner. There are several notable exceptions, but, sadly, too few of them write for the big-circulation papers.

So exit Di Canio, and enter Blinker. Regi is a delightful character, and he came very close early on to being a huge Celtic favourite. Sadly, though, after twenty minutes of sheer magic against Motherwell at Celtic Park in November, he was red-carded for an elbowing offence. Celtic lost that match – unbelievably, on the evidence of the opening twenty minutes – and Regi has fought something of a battle with the fans ever since, although his performances latterly under Jozef Venglos may enable him to win that battle.

But one headache had been removed in the form of Paolo Di Canio. His departure ended up giving me substantial personal grief from the press, although the board appeared delighted that we had extricated ourselves from a very difficult situation by bringing in a player the head coach wanted while generating a massive profit on Di Canio.

As such considerations do not appear to weigh heavily with the fans, there was undoubtedly some disappointment about his departure. This was shared by me. I would have loved to have seen him play alongside the likes of Henrik Larsson, Craig Burley and Paul Lambert, but there is no doubt that Paolo himself did not have that on his agenda.

But life was still tough. Another headache remained. His name was Jorge Cadete.

CHAPTER 4

Time to Strengthen

Not only was the Celtic coaching staff decimated by the end of season 1996–97, the playing staff too required urgent refurbishing. The saddest single aspect had been the loss of Paul McStay, whose career was ended prematurely by an ankle injury when he was only 32. Having lost John Collins under the Bosman ruling one year earlier, losing McStay at this time was a severe blow, especially when the sands of time at Celtic had run out for excellent servants like Peter Grant and Brian O'Neil and in the midfield area fine players like Phil O'Donnell and Morten Wieghorst had been severely hampered by injury. Decisions also had to be taken about out-of-contract players like Tosh McKinlay and Malky Mackay.

The recruiting of the previous season had seen the arrival of Paolo Di Canio, Tommy Johnson from Aston Villa, Alan Stubbs from Bolton Wanderers and David Hannah from Dundee United. It was clear, however, that a major overhaul was urgently required, and one minus side to the hiring of Wim Jansen was the fact that he was not as up to speed with the current scene in Britain and in Europe as he might have been in an ideal situation because of the time he had recently spent in Japan. However, the club was able to depend on the expertise of Davie Hay as chief scout and I believed that the engagement of Murdo MacLeod as number two would be of considerable assistance, especially as far as the Scottish scene was concerned.

Jansen's men, Larsson and Blinker, were instantly targeted, with a series of meetings taking place involving the head coach, Murdo MacLeod and Davie Hay with a view to establishing what other players should be pursued. This was all done in the context of Wim being allowed to assess the existing staff to establish the areas which required strengthening.

Fairly early in this process, I suppose I should have been alerted to troubles ahead.

'You lied to me,' Wim told me one day.

'In what way?' I asked, not being aware of anything which could give rise to such a comment.

'You told me we had a lot of good players at the club, but we don't,' he replied.

'Yes, I did say that, and one or two international managers appear to agree with me,' I replied. 'I also said that it was up to you to make the players into a team and that there would be substantial funds available to enable you to strengthen the squad.'

Strengthening the squad was a matter of immense priority, not least to me. It has always intrigued me why people should think that I had any interest in delaying transfers to the club. No one had a greater incentive than I had to bring in new players since I would certainly be in the firing line if none arrived.

Endless discussions took place to decide which players should be pursued. I saw my role as being the observer who simply asked questions without offering any technical opinion since I was not qualified to provide any. Strangely enough, Davie Hay constantly asked me to express an opinion but the few words of advice from my brother Craig at the start of this great adventure kept reverberating around my head. 'Make sure that you don't give any technical football opinions,' he told me. 'They are liable to come back and haunt you.' This was excellent advice which I remained determined to follow throughout my time at the club.

My relationship with my older brother has always been excellent. Despite the six-year age gap, which he constantly tries to conceal, we have always been close. He is a man who gives serious advice sparingly. When he gives it, my experience tells me that he is well worth listening to. After all, it was his advice which stopped me attempting what would have been an unsuccessful bid to forge a career as a professional footballer!

Davie Hay certainly put me under pressure on a number of occasions to compromise on that advice. Not for a moment do I think he did so in anything but the best of spirit, and we normally had that type of discussion on a one-to-one basis.

There is no question, though, that I did ask a lot of questions about players who were mentioned. My concern on behalf of the club was to ensure that any signing made sense in providing value for money and also fitted in with a general overall policy to attempt to reduce the average age of the squad.

Contract management post-Bosman is an essential element of every major club's organisation. It is not only important simply to identify a good player. Consideration also has to be given to his effect on the overall financial position of the club. In simple terms, paying huge sums of money for a player in the twilight of his career is seldom commercially sensible, since you are effectively writing off every penny you spend without any prospect of a return. The exception would be in circumstances where a player of that type provided the final piece in a team's jigsaw or was likely to provide such immense playing value during his time at the club that the write-off was justified.

Because of my background as a football commentator I have a very fair knowledge of the statistics affecting any player. At the time of my arrival at Celtic I could have told you the dates of birth of a very large percentage of the players in the Scottish Football League. I could also tell you their background in terms of previous clubs and involvement in first-team play. Indeed, that type of statistical information had been sought from me on a regular basis by a number of Scottish managers, especially at the time of transfer negotiations. I kept books and records about clubs and players every season of my commentating career.

Accordingly, no one needed to tell me that Darren Jackson was born on 25 July 1966. Giving him a three-year contract at the age of 31 flew somewhat in the face of overall policy but there was general agreement between Davie Hay and Murdo MacLeod that Jackson would be a valuable acquisition to the club in terms of skill, restless energy, commitment and spirit. His recent arrival on the international scene had also given him a new lease of life, and he had made himself one of the fittest players in the country with the kind of enthusiasm which would ensure that he was in effect offering the talents of a much younger man.

Darren became Wim Jansen's first signing, although the head coach had never seen him play. He was happy to depend on the advice given by his trusted lieutenants. Mind you, I was firmly of the opinion that he had watched him on tape and said so at the signing press conference. Wim later corrected me and told me that I should not have said that he had watched Jackson on video because he hadn't. I certainly felt that he should have done, because tapes were readily available.

The reason Darren was the first signing was the delay in the arrival of Henrik Larsson from Feyenoord. He had a clause in his contract with the Dutch club enabling him to leave should a specific, and modest, price be offered by another club for his services. We offered that price and obtained authority to speak to him about personal terms, which Davie Hay and I did in Holland. Agreement was readily achieved but then Feyenoord became upset, particularly with Henrik's agent. A legal battle ensued in Holland to establish that the vital clause in the contract was enforceable, leaving Henrik free to join Celtic. That involved a delay of some two to three weeks, but the legal argument was won and Celtic had an outstanding player.

The fact that both Darren Jackson and Henrik Larsson had proved themselves versatile in their careers at both club and international level was a significant bonus in bringing them to Celtic. Both had played in midfield and up front for their country, although both were brought to the club principally for their attacking skills.

A natural midfield powerhouse was still essential, particularly in the absence of the unlucky Paul McStay. Discussions narrowed down to two players, one of whom was Craig Burley of Chelsea, better known to Scottish supporters at that time as a wing-back in the international team but well known to relevant people at Celtic as a natural central midfield player.

My contribution to the debate about the two players was simple. 'Let's imagine we are playing Rangers at Ibrox,' I said. 'We are a goal down playing against the wind and rain and the referee is an out-and-out homer. Which of these two players would make a greater impact on the proceedings for Celtic?'

I was offering no opinion, but was keen to know the professionals' verdict. Davie Hay and Murdo MacLeod agreed instantly. Craig Burley arrived from Chelsea shortly afterwards.

Decisions were also taken about Tosh McKinlay and Malky Mackay. Both were re-signed. The end of the Celtic road arrived for Brian O'Neil, Peter Grant and Chris Hay, who were transferred to Aberdeen, Norwich City and Swindon Town respectively. They had been around the Celtic scene for many years and had given valuable service. They left in one sense with heavy hearts, but they all realised that it was time to go. They departed with dignity and honour and with the best wishes of everyone at the club.

Tosh McKinlay had been re-signed despite Davie Hay's great enthusiasm for bringing in Stephane Mahe from Rennes. It was made clear to Tosh at the time of his re-signing negotiations that another left-back was under consideration but Tosh was more than willing to stand his corner and fight for his Celtic career. In these days of commercialism and constant movement of players, if you were choosing a team of Celtic players over the years who would 'play for the jersey', Tosh would be in the starting line-up.

The pursuit of Stephane Mahe ended successfully and I had my first experience of dealing with a foreign player whose English was worse than my French. That presented some settling-in difficulties for Stephane but within a short period of time he had been fully integrated and was a key member of the rapidly reshaped Celtic team.

By that time the matches had started in earnest. After a thoroughly forgettable Umbro tournament in Ireland there was more encouragement from decent pre-season-friendly performances against Parma and Roma, but the first two league matches brought gloom and despondency and, indeed, calls for Wim Jansen's head.

Wim's preferred system at the outset was a 3–4–3 formation with the front three consisting of two wingers and a central striker. The problem was that we didn't have players on the staff who could fit into such a system readily and that was apparent in the first league match against Hibernian. This was a match dominated by Chick Charnley, who accepted the freedom of Easter Road that afternoon to inflict enough damage on Celtic to create a 2–1 defeat.

Henrik Larsson came on as a second-half substitute playing wide on the left and his only memorable contribution was to give the ball to Chick Charnley to shoot home the winning goal. Happily, Henrik has scarcely put a foot out of place since and must be one of the best pound-for-pound buys in Celtic's history.

That match also marked the end of Gordon Marshall's time as first-team goalkeeper at the club. Following the departures of Peter Grant and Paul McStay, Marshall had become the longest-serving Celtic player still at the club, having been signed from Falkirk in 1991. Having given excellent service, he had become one of those unfortunate players who couldn't get a break from the Celtic supporters. Peter Grant finished up in that category, and Darren Jackson acquired similar status later. Injury had kept Stewart Kerr on the sidelines and now a real crisis emerged with an injury to Marshall. While his injury was short term, Stewart's was longer term and the European deadline was fast approaching.

By the Thursday of the following week the goalkeeping crisis was at its height. Virtually the whole afternoon was devoted to considering our options with regard to bringing in cover for Gordon Marshall and Stewart Kerr, especially with Europe in mind. We all departed on the Thursday evening with the situation unresolved.

Early the next morning I received a telephone call from Bobby Gould, the manager of Wales. 'I hear you have a goalkeeping problem,' he said. 'If so, my son Jonathan would be available immediately from Bradford City and I am sure he wouldn't let you down.'

I remembered Jonathan from a lengthy spell in Coventry City's goal while Steve Ogrizovic was injured. During that spell he was brought into the Scotland squad and it had looked as though his career was on the up and up. However, Ogrizovic had returned and I had lost track of Jonathan's progress.

I immediately went to the coach's room, where Wim, Murdo and Davie had gathered. They were still discussing goalkeepers and I asked them simply if they wanted Jonathan Gould. Wim could offer no opinion. However, Murdo and Davie looked at each other, nodded and indicated that, in the circumstances, Jonathan was as good a bet as any.

I called Jonathan on his mobile phone at the training ground in Bradford to establish his precise position. He confirmed that he had agreed with Chris Kamara, the Bradford City manager, that if he could find another club then he could go for no fee, except that the new club would have to assume responsibility for the one outstanding instalment on his signing-on fee. I told him I would contact the club formally since time was of the essence and that he was wanted as number three goalkeeper. He had to be signed that day.

Jonathan indicated that he would speak to his manager, leave the training ground and head for Glasgow immediately in his car. Having cleared the position with the club, I then negotiated Jonathan's terms over his mobile as he travelled north. The contract was prepared while he was still *en route* and I arranged for the club doctor to be available to meet him on arrival to give him what was, by Celtic's standards, a cursory medical. It was made perfectly clear to Jonathan that he would be behind Gordon Marshall and Stewart Kerr in the goalkeeping queue, although he was likely to have an early opportunity because of injuries.

By 4.30 p.m. that Friday afternoon, Jonathan had been signed and international clearance had been obtained. He made his debut immediately and played seventy consecutive first-team matches before a knee injury sustained in Zurich forced him out at the beginning of November 1998. He must rival Henrik Larsson as a top value-for-money signing. There were very few things during my time at Celtic which gave me more pleasure than reaching him on that same mobile telephone in May 1998 to tell him that he had been called into the Scotland World Cup squad to replace Andy Goram.

Referring back to that job description, I also had overall responsibility for youth development and I had become firmly of the view that the traditional system of having both a reserve-team coach and a youth-team coach on a hierarchical basis was outdated. What I thought was required was an overall development system dealing with all matters outwith the first-team squad and under the overall control of one manager, with a team of coaches working under him, dealing with all the junior teams at the club and ensuring that there was continuity and consistency of approach in the development of players.

I discussed this at length with the head youth coach, Willie McStay. We agreed that it was almost certain that reserve-team football was on the way out and that an under-age system would replace it. In these circumstances, the development plan which I had in mind made sense.

Willie's coaching credentials are excellent. He took a big chance after his playing career ended in taking over as manager of Sligo Rovers in Ireland, and on the back of his success there was brought to Celtic Park by Tommy Burns. He is very highly respected in coaching circles, particularly for his work on the training ground, and I found him committed, switched on and a pleasure to work with. He was certainly the man I had in mind to be development manager.

However, all this meant nothing unless the overall proposal had the blessing of the head coach. I discussed the matter in some detail with Wim and Murdo, since it was virtually impossible to discuss anything with Wim without Murdo's presence. They both sanctioned the overall plan and, indeed, expressed enthusiasm. However, when I indicated that I had Willie McStay in mind for the post, Murdo gave that idea the thumbs down. I am not entirely sure what the reason for this was, although I do recall Murdo making some reference to Willie being an 'empire-builder'.

It didn't really matter. Wim clearly supported Murdo in his opinion (didn't he always?). The view I took was that without the complete blessing of the head coach and his number two, the appointment of Willie as development manager was a non-starter. An alternative had to be found. An invitation to Wim and Murdo to provide suggestions bore no fruit, but I reflected very carefully on the matter and remembered a conversation I had had with my brother Craig the previous season when travelling to a match with him. Simply by way of conversation I had asked him who he considered to be best of the new generation of up-and-coming coaches. He mentioned several names and indicated that one he thought might go as far as any was a young coach he had on his staff at the Scottish Football Association. The name was Eric Black.

I put that name to Murdo and Wim. 'Yes, he is a good man,' said Murdo. 'You'd like him, Wim.'

Eric's playing career at Aberdeen and Metz was explained to Wim and

I was readily given approval to open discussions with Eric. That meant, of course, a telephone call to Craig, which went down like a lead balloon. He told me he had wondered how long it would be before I made that call, since he, too, recollected the conversation of the previous season and realised that in my new role, with a heavily depleted coaching staff at Celtic, it was likely that such a call would be made. Happily, there was nothing contractually preventing Eric from talking to me, although Craig insisted on speaking to him first to establish interest and, no doubt, to try to persuade him to stay at Park Gardens.

I had only met Eric fairly briefly on two or three previous occasions but eventually had the chance to discuss the Celtic situation in detail. After these discussions, and having made a number of other enquiries, I was satisfied that Eric was the man for the job. I explained to him, however, that no appointment could be considered without the approval of the head coach, and I set up an interview, which I did not attend, involving Eric, Wim and Murdo. This took place in the Hilton Hotel in Glasgow on a Wednesday evening and apparently lasted some one and a half hours.

The following morning Wim and Murdo confirmed that they would be happy to have Eric as development manager and that I should attempt to negotiate terms. This was duly done and Eric came on board at the end of August 1997. Fortunately, he was delighted to have the opportunity to work with Willie McStay, who would remain in his capacity as head youth coach, although now answerable to Eric rather than the old-style manager.

Willie had read the script. He realised that an outside factor had prevented his appointment as development manager, and while I remained silent on the issue as far as he was concerned, I was aware that he had identified Murdo as his likely saboteur. He confirmed this to me much later. However, Willie curbed his obvious disappointment superbly and conducted himself with the utmost integrity as he adjusted to his new role working beside Eric. My own view was that we had an outstanding partnership in charge of our youth development, and that remains my belief.

Sadly for Eric, Willie and the others in the development department, the honeymoon with the head coach and assistant head coach never actually took place. Virtually from day one Eric and Willie were ostracised by Murdo and hence, of course, by Wim.

When it came to trying to liaise, co-operate and relate to the head coach and assistant head coach, the lives of Eric Black and Willie McStay became a misery. The reasons are, for me, still not totally clear.

I began reading veiled suggestions in newspapers that I had appointed Eric Black without the consent of Wim and Murdo, but I knew this not to be the case.

The only possible reason I can think of for Murdo reacting to the arrival of Eric Black in such a fashion became apparent a little later. It appears that Murdo formed the view – wrongly – that Eric was receiving a better salary than he was. Yes, I realise that this should not be a reason for Murdo to make Eric feel like a leper, but there is no doubt that Murdo believed Eric's salary was higher and that he was bitterly offended. A fateful meeting between Murdo and me in October brought all that into the clear and gave me the plainest possible indication that the appointment of Murdo MacLeod had been the biggest single mistake of my time at Celtic.

It was certainly not a mistake, however, to accede to Eric Black's request to bring in Kenny McDowall and Tom O'Neill as development coaches, although the sad aspect of the recruiting was the need to dispense with the services of Danny Crainie, a man with whom I had no grievance at all but who was not felt to fit into the development team which was being established.

CHAPTER 5

Exit Cadete

Jorge Cadete's house was magnificent. It was situated some 40 miles out of Lisbon and while the area in which it sat left something to be desired, the residence itself was something special. Jorge was immensely proud of it, and little wonder. From the moment you negotiated the electric security gates until the moment you departed, everything was top class. There was an orchard in the garden and a swimming pool. Dog kennels provided better accommodation than many people occupying the inner city of Lisbon were able to enjoy. The house itself was immaculate.

What was somewhat disconcerting, however, was the fact that virtually throughout the two and a half hours I spent as his guest, a video ran displaying a series of goals scored by Jorge in his career. The video ran in a loop so that the array of goals was relentless. Jorge could tell you the where, when and how of each of them. Whether it was a second-leg UEFA Cup tie in Poland in 1991 or an international goal for Portugal made no difference to him. He could tell you every detail about each. What he couldn't do, however, was reconcile himself to playing for Celtic and enhance his already legendary status. He really did score goals for fun. But not much about Jorge's life, apart from that, appeared to be fun.

To be fair, he was the perfect host. Eric Riley, the club's financial director, and I followed Dr Jack Mulhearn to Portugal to investigate the prospects of bringing him back to Celtic Park. He hadn't reported back for pre-season training and had sent through his agents medical certificates suggesting a depressive illness and psychological dif-ficulties. I have often wondered what Jock Stein, Bill Shankly and Sir Matt Busby would have made of references from footballers to stress and emotional and psychological problems.

Dr Mulhearn had a good relationship with Jorge, as he has with all the players at Celtic as far as I am aware. We wanted Jorge checked out and we were confident that he would submit himself to the doctor's examination willingly. He did so, and Dr Mulhearn was able to confirm that there was a genuine health problem which needed to be addressed.

Eric Riley and I were anxious to establish whether or not we could assist in creating an environment whereby Jorge could return and continue providing the goals which appeared to come so naturally to him. He greeted us graciously, showed us around his magnificent home and generally extended excellent hospitality. For me this was a new experience. I had not dealt with Jorge before and was effectively meeting him for the first time. I liked him. He was certainly different and I could understand why he had become something of a loner in Glasgow, but he certainly had likeable qualities and did appear to be genuinely concerned about the whole situation.

It became apparent that he had suffered difficulties in Glasgow. He was obviously a man who required a great deal of attention, although he was unlikely to ask for this. He also tended to keep grievances to himself. He certainly believed that he was underpaid. He had formed the view that other players in the Celtic squad were earning better salaries than he was commanding and he believed that, as a top striker, he should be among the best-paid players at the club, if not the best-paid player.

We made it clear that he was very much wanted in Glasgow and that we would consider carefully all the points he had made. His agent and lawyer were present and I had ongoing discussions with them in which I proposed a new, extended, improved deal.

About a week after the initial visit I had further detailed discussions with his agent and lawyer as a result of which we were able to agree in principle a new contract. It transpired, however, that Jorge's wife was a major stumbling block. She had no desire to leave either Portugal, or their house outside Lisbon. She was not at home initially while Eric and I were visiting but she arrived back at the house while we were still there. Strangely, she never came through to meet us but remained in another part of the house while occasionally shouting through to Jorge to have him leave us to speak to her. Clearly, this was not a healthy sign.

Sure enough, on the morning after I thought terms had been agreed with Jorge's representatives, I received several calls from Jorge on my mobile telephone explaining to me that his wife was still not prepared to come to Glasgow and that in these circumstances he could not take up the new deal. He sounded genuinely apologetic.

I was bitterly disappointed. Our attitude had been that it was entirely appropriate for a new deal to be put to Jorge involving better financial terms so long as an extended period of the contract was also incorporated.

Once again, the directors were entirely supportive. They accepted completely the argument that we needed a top-class striker and that Jorge represented little risk so long as we could have him settled in Glasgow. Without him, we had to go into the market place with all the attendant risks and would certainly have to pay a higher salary than Jorge was originally enjoying.

The logic of these arguments was readily accepted by the directors, especially in view of the fact that there is a huge shortage of guaranteed strikers available. Think about it – Alex Ferguson at Manchester United took a very long time to complete the deal which brought Dwight Yorke from Aston Villa at a reported price in excess of £12 million. Within that period, he was linked with Marcelo Salas, the Chilean striker who eventually signed for Lazio. One huge disincentive to purchasing a South American star is the fact he is liable to spend so much of his time in the air flying across the Atlantic to play for his national team that you have to accept that you may be without him for the best part of twelve weeks a year. The shortage of top-class strikers was such, though, that in Manchester United's case a huge sum was necessary to prise Yorke from Aston Villa.

Similarly, shortly after George Graham took over as manager of Tottenham Hotspur in October 1998, he indicated that such was the shortage of top-class players to bring to the club that it might be February 1999 before he was able to freshen up his squad significantly. This was greeted with scarcely a murmur, simply quiet nods of heads confirming difficulty. Can you imagine the reaction if such a statement had been issued by anyone at Celtic?

So, with great reluctance, we had to accept that Cadete would have to be transferred, but the possible buyers were heavily restricted. He wanted to go to a club from which he could commute to his palatial home outside Lisbon. Having become *persona non grata* at Sporting Lisbon, the prospects at that time of Benfica being interested were slim, and Porto were certainly blessed with top-class strikers.

Eventually, the possibility of a move to Celta Vigo came to the fore. At last, Jorge was interested. Informal approaches from English Premiership clubs had been rejected out of hand and the arrival of Celta Vigo on the scene was a real bonus, bearing in mind the possibility of Jorge reflecting dead money as he languished in his Portuguese pad. Our bargaining power was, of course, heavily restricted. I spent a difficult weekend in London with the officials from Celta Vigo trying to agree terms to enable Jorge to be transferred, and after much ado a deal was agreed on terms which reflected a healthy profit for Celtic but scarcely represented value for his undoubted scoring prowess.

However, it transpired that the discount necessitated by Jorge's psychological difficulties was appropriate. He played precious few games for the Spanish club and eventually fell into dispute with them before moving on to Benfica.

So the third of the hallowed trio had gone. Between them, Pierre Van Hooijdonk, Paolo Di Canio and Jorge Cadete generated endless criticism for the management at Celtic. Fergus McCann was pilloried for alleged mismanagement of Pierre Van Hooijdonk before my time, and I took relentless stick, along with Fergus, over Di Canio and Cadete. For a while these were the only two subjects raised by the press on a day-to-day basis, apart from whom we were going to sign.

Yet Van Hooijdonk proved to be a nightmare to Nottingham Forest; Di Canio ended up assaulting a referee at Sheffield Wednesday before going absent without leave; and Jorge Cadete continued a course of conduct which had seen him in serious dispute with Sporting Lisbon before arriving at Celtic and then continuing in a similar vein with Celta Vigo. It was always a matter of great amazement to me that Celtic appeared to carry all the blame for the difficulties with these players while they were in Glasgow, despite the evidence suggesting that the players were the problem. Apparently that does not make as attractive copy as the other way around.

It did have an effect on the club's approach to new signings. It was not enough for us to establish that potential recruits had the kind of ability which would improve the team, we also had to do as much as possible by way of background research to establish whether or not we were bringing serious problems to the club. In that respect, I think we were successful during my time. It is also worth reflecting that despite the hero status afforded to Van Hooijdonk, Di Canio and Cadete, only one of them left Scotland with a medal of any kind, and that was Van Hooijdonk after the Scottish Cup win in 1995. It is always extremely difficult to calculate the disruptive effect within the dressing-room, and within the club generally, of players causing problems, but the evidence of that particular trio suggests that while they were all outstanding players in their own right, their effect on team success was less than it ought to have been.

Shortly after Cadete's departure to Spain, a prominent article appeared in the Glasgow *Evening Times* which purported to explain precisely the deal I had offered the player. It set out in very substantial detail the contract proposal. The article, in fact, contained about two dozen points of 'fact'. All but two were wrong. The two which were correct were that the term of the contract offered was four years (I suppose that was a reasonable guess on anyone's part) and that he would receive the same bonuses as the rest of the players, which again would not have been hard to deduce. No one from the newspaper contacted me or any other club official to check out the story. It was so inaccurate that it couldn't have come from anyone who was privy to the information. Indeed, I was the only person at Celtic who knew every detail of the contract proposal, with the board not requiring to be informed because the deal foundered.

Around the same time, another article appeared in the same newspaper which set out to explain that Rangers and Celtic were now in the big league as far as players' salaries were concerned. The import was that Rangers and Celtic were matching the English Premiership in terms of the scale of contracts offered to top players. The article then went on to identify the best-paid players at each club and the salaries they were receiving. Every single detail relating to Celtic was wrong, so I find it difficult to imagine that there was any more accuracy in the part of the story relating to Rangers. In any event, anyone calculating the total salaries claimed to be given to the top eight players at Rangers against the total salary bill as shown in the Rangers accounts would discover that international players not in the top eight must have been earning balloons and goldfish.

Both these articles were in a sense flattering both to Celtic and, in the case of Cadete, to me, but that is irrelevant. The more important factor is the level of misinformation to which clubs like Rangers and Celtic are subjected on too frequent a basis. The tragedy is, a huge percentage of the public appears to believe that if something appears in print it must be true. There is also a common belief that there is no smoke without fire. I can assure you from my personal experiences that there is lots and lots of smoke without any fire as far as some of the media coverage of football in Glasgow is concerned.

One consistent way to generate such smoke is for journalists to indicate to managers, coaches or players that someone else has said something derogatory about them, with the helpful scribe then offering the right of reply. Suddenly you are tempted to comment or respond to allegations which have never been made. If you are daft enough to fall for that one, that gives the same scribe the opportunity to go to the original 'culprit' and keep the whole game running. If you respond to the original enquiry by suggesting that you are not prepared to comment on something you have not heard first hand, the unscrupulous journalist can take personal offence and see that as a reason for carving you up. It is frightening.

CHAPTER 6
_____

Enter Lambert

David Hay went on holiday in the second fortnight of August 1997. He gave forty-eight hours' notice of departing for the sun in Cyprus and one of the results was that I was left with an office to myself.

By the time I arrived at Celtic Park, decisions had already been taken about relocating the entire administration staff to new offices in the south-east corner of the stadium. The space was at a premium and I was happy to agree to share an office with Davie. However, the location was a long way from the football nerve centre in the south stand. It was obvious to me instantly that the geography was not conducive to building the necessary bridges between administration, management and playing and technical staff in the manner desired.

Originally, it was expected that the head coach and back-up coaching staff would also relocate to the south-east corner. There was not one chance in a hundred of that working. To attempt to withdraw football coaching staff from the dressing-room area to offices close to directors and senior management was wholly unrealistic. In this respect I agreed totally with Wim Jansen, who point-blank refused to have anything to do with occupying offices away from the football area.

Mind you, it would not have done any harm for him to communicate the solid reasons for adopting this position. Communication with the executives and administration staff was certainly not Wim's strong point. I made it clear to the directors that the proposal would not work and I saw no merit whatsoever in attempting to persuade Wim and the coaches to relocate. My preferred view was that David Hay and I should also vacate the south-east corner and rejoin the football staff in the south stand. There was considerable resistance to that viewpoint and it took several months for what I considered to be the necessary relocation to take place. By that time, sadly, Davie Hay had gone. In effect, however, Davie took his leave of the south-east corner almost immediately, since after a very short period of time he seldom utilised his office space.

By the time Davie went on holiday there had been considerable discussion about Paul Lambert. He had certainly been among the names on Davie Hay's dossier right from the outset and he appealed to Wim Jansen principally because of his European Cup success with Borussia Dortmund the previous season.

Paul Lambert had been the subject of debate within Celtic for the best part of two years. While he was at Motherwell he was watched very closely indeed with a view to bringing him to Celtic Park and, indeed, I believe an attempt was made to purchase him, although it was obviously not one made with total conviction since Motherwell's financial position combined with Lambert's impending Bosman status would surely have made a deal none too difficult to conclude if there had been a concerted will.

In order not to complicate the situation it was preferable that Lambert remained with Borussia Dortmund until 10 August 1997, by which time he would have completed one year with the German team. Any transfer within that period meant that Motherwell retained rights to a share of the transfer fee. Fergus McCann told me later that he had attempted to bring Lambert to Celtic Park when Tommy Burns was manager and even reached agreement on a payment to Motherwell in the event that a deal could be struck with Borussia Dortmund. But agreement with the German club couldn't be achieved. They wanted him to stay.

In the event that this position might change, it was, however, clearly advisable for Wim to see Lambert play. This was consistent with the club policy of seeing players live when significant money was involved. We had already departed from that policy in respect of earlier deals because of the urgency of the situation but there was now no impediment to Wim checking out Lambert's skills, which he eventually did in Aberdeen when Scotland played Belarus. By that time I had already made overtures to Borussia Dortmund about the availability of Lambert and it had been made perfectly plain to me that they still wanted him to stay in Germany. Indeed, the initial position adopted by Borussia Dortmund was that he was not available. They would not even quote a price.

However, Paul's agent at that time, Jim Melrose, was constantly in touch with Celtic, usually via Davie Hay, making it clear that Paul was desperate to return to Scotland and, indeed, required to do so on compassionate grounds. Shortly before his international appearance,

Paul appeared on BBC's *Sportscene* and started making comments like, 'I don't care what Jock Brown thinks about me. It doesn't matter if he doesn't rate me because Ottmar Hitzfeld and Craig Brown obviously think well enough of me.'

He went on to mention my name on two or three occasions, having clearly formed the impression that I did not rate him and was not prepared to purchase him. Nothing was further from the truth. What bemused me, however, was the basis upon which he was making these observations. I cast my mind back carefully over the time he was the subject of interest within the club and could not recall at any time even passing an opinion on him. As it happens, I think he is an excellent player and have always thought so. I thought he should have moved directly from Motherwell to Celtic since he would have been an ideal player to have brought in at the time when Paul McStay and Peter Grant were coming to the end of their Celtic careers – not that my view matters.

People started asking me how I rated Paul Lambert. It was only after the matter had been contemplated for some time that I had a flash of inspiration. Davie Hay returned from holiday. On one of the very rare occasions when he sat across from me in our office, I asked him if he had, by any chance, told Jim Melrose that I did not rate Paul Lambert. 'As a matter of fact, I did,' said Davie. 'I am sorry. I was being pestered to death by Mello and I just told him that to get him off the phone.'

'Thanks very much,' I said. 'Do you realise that Paul has been all over television telling everyone I don't rate him?'

Davie apologised profusely. I do not believe for one moment that he was trying to do me any harm, nor was he trying to damage Paul Lambert. Jim Melrose is as likeable a guy as you could hope to meet but he had the persistence of a bulldog when he sensed the possibility of one of his clients making a move. I have no doubt that Davie was under considerable pressure. Unfortunately, though, while Davie's observations to Melrose prior to disappearing on holiday solved his particular problem, it caused me a problem which continued to reverberate until the day I left Celtic.

In any event, with Wim having watched Paul at first hand, I doubled my efforts to persuade Borussia Dortmund to release him. They conducted themselves totally honourably and quite properly but were firm in their resolve to try to persuade Paul that his future lay in Germany. I still could not get them to quote me a price. However, pressure began to be applied directly by Paul in Dortmund and as a result the club began to weaken. I was then told that they would consider a deal after the Champions' League matches had been completed. That would be in the second week of December. Clearly, Paul was totally unhappy about that and continued applying pressure at the German end.

Eventually Borussia Dortmund started to talk about money. After some haggling, a price was agreed and I was given a date when Paul could come to Glasgow. This was scheduled to be immediately after a Champions' League match in November. I was given authority to discuss personal terms with Jim Melrose to bring Paul to Celtic and met him in the north of England to conclude negotiations. A deal was in place.

However, the day before what was to be Paul's final match for Borussia Dortmund, I received a telephone call from their general manager, Michael Meier, who conducted proceedings for them, to the effect that they were going to make one last concerted effort that day to persuade Paul to stay. I protested that everything had been agreed, including his personal terms, and that this was surely now inappropriate.

Mr Meier, who conducted himself in a gentlemanly manner at all times, acknowledged that this was the case but felt that he had to make one last attempt to do what he believed to be right for his club, although he thought he should tell me in advance that he was going to do this. I respected that. I then had to depend on Paul Lambert's determination to come to Celtic to ensure that the deal went through. Happily, Paul delivered. He received a hero's farewell in Dortmund and travelled to Glasgow on the Thursday to complete the formalities necessary to become a Celtic player.

Accusations were later made to the effect that I had delayed the transfer because I did not rate him as a player. Utter nonsense. I did everything in my power to bring him to the club at the earliest possible opportunity and was very pleased indeed that my persistence paid off.

Where I was less than forthcoming, however, was in keeping Wim Jansen fully informed of the developments in negotiations. Wim basically showed no interest whatsoever in the details of any of the transactions to bring players to the club. He seldom sought any information about ongoing negotiations. I took a lead from that and failed to volunteer any more information than was apparently wanted. Once the player was identified, Wim simply wanted him in the dressing-room as a Celtic player. I was perfectly happy about that. The impression I had was that he had no interest whatsoever in a blow-by-blow account of procedures involved in making that happen. These procedures are frequently very complicated, especially when you have to deal with agents acting for the selling club, agents acting for the targeted player and the relentless enquiries made by the media, not only about a player of genuine interest but frequently about several others who are not in the frame.

There was one other significant factor. One of my tasks was to seal off leaks of information from the club. One way to do that was to operate on a need-to-know basis and not offer gratuitous information. Make no mistake, I trusted Wim Jansen. However, he was certainly not demanding as far as seeking information was concerned. Perhaps I overdid keeping my cards close to my chest in the interests of confidentiality, but I regret that I felt the overall situation dictated this.

When Paul Lambert arrived in Glasgow, he could not have been more pleasant and I remember joking with him about the allegations he had obviously heard about me not rating him as a player. There was absolutely no problem whatsoever between us. Sadly, that was to change.

CHAPTER 7

The Courage of Darren Jackson

It's as if they grow on trees.

'Sign a striker, why don't you sign a striker?'

The implication was that any striker would do as long as he was a household name and cost a fortune. I gained the impression that a three-legged Martian would have appeased the press, and therefore a huge percentage of the Celtic supporters, as long as he passed these tests. Obviously, if he couldn't play, he would simply need to be replaced and the clamour would begin for yet another striker.

The fact that the club had three current international strikers on its books, together with a top-class Premiership striker in Tommy Johnson, who was injured, meant nothing. The loudest sections of the press demanded that we sign a striker. That clamour continued, notwithstanding the fact that Henrik Larsson and Simon Donnelly formed a very effective striking partnership which had been a key element of a long successful run from September through to November.

Poor Simon Donnelly never seemed to receive the credit he deserved. Perhaps it was because he had come through the ranks and had not been purchased at a substantial price. Nevertheless, he scored important goal after important goal and linked up superbly with Larsson during that spell, prompted from the middle of the field by Craig Burley and Morten Wieghorst. Larsson, understandably, had become something of a hero, and not just because of his eccentric coiffure. He was the man, above all others, who was capable of providing what a world-renowned coach once described to me as 'the surprising moment'.

Admittedly, we were thin on the ground if anything happened to Larsson and Donnelly during that spell. Tommy Johnson was a long-erm casualty, sidelined with a serious knee injury. But the night of the UEFA Cup return leg against FC Tirol at the end of August really created a major stir throughout the club. Trailing 2–1 from the first leg in Austria, the team was travelling up in the coach from the pre-match hotel when Darren Jackson began to feel unwell. He had a severe headache and a feeling of nausea. By the time he arrived at the stadium, the main problem was the headache. He asked to see the club doctor, Jack Mulhearn. After close examination, Jack indicated that he was not happy and that Darren should be withdrawn from the team.

To Wim Jansen's great credit, he accepted instantly the recommendation of the doctor and applied no pressure whatsoever on Jackson to play. It was not hard to imagine the number of tough managers who might have said, 'A headache? You want to call off with a headache? Get your kit on, you are playing.' Not Jansen. He always showed immense respect for the medical advice he received from Jack and from Brian Scott, the physio. There was no argument, Darren was out.

The ailment he was suffering from could scarcely have been alleviated by the events of that particular night. Simon Donnelly volleyed home a marvellous opening goal after about half an hour and at that point, if things stayed the same, we were through on the away-goals rule. The Austrians equalised. We were out. We went 2–1 up, which could have meant extra time. The Austrians equalised again just on half-time. We were out. Then came a forty-five-minute performance which for me dispelled any lingering doubts about the supreme quality of Henrik Larsson. He made it abundantly clear right from the kick-off that he was not prepared to end up on the losing side. He was everywhere. He created opening after opening and inspired the team to obtain the two goals necessary to go through. Then he, like everyone else in the packed stadium, watched in anguish as the Austrians scored again to make the score on the night 4–3 and give them the advantage on the away-goals rule.

There followed more Larsson-inspired magic and concerted determination by the whole team, and Morten Wieghorst scored the fifth about five minutes from the end. Still the roller-coaster was riveting. The Austrians pressed for a fourth goal which would take them through. Then Larsson picked the ball up around the halfway line on the left-hand side and took the ball for a wander. He went past player after player towards the corner flag and then decided to move inside. As he did so, Craig Burley surged from the midfield unmarked,

Larsson laid the ball on a plate and Burley stroked home goal number six to end the torture.

Sitting in the directors' box watching with mixed emotions was Darren Jackson. The headache still troubled him. He was ordered home as quickly as possible with the instruction that he should call Jack Mulhearn the next morning if the pain-killing tablets had not had the desired effect. Sadly, after a torturous night he called the doctor and arrangements were made immediately for him to have a brain scan. Happily for Darren and the club, this was an area in which Jack Mulhearn had specific knowledge, much of it gained from personal experience. His medical instincts told him something serious was amiss. Darren was not regularly affected by headaches. The nature of the symptoms troubled the doctor.

That afternoon, following the scan, I received a call from Brian Scott indicating that all was not well. There appeared to be a potentially serious problem. Darren was required to return to the hospital the following morning for further tests and it appeared that not only was his career in doubt, but his life might be threatened. I had to arrange for him to attend hospital for the additional tests the following morning, without alarming him needlessly. I spoke to him at home and indicated that the tests had not proved conclusive and therefore, to be on the safe side, a further test should be carried out. I tried very hard to appear calm and untroubled. What Darren thought overnight I am not sure. He is, by nature, something of a worrier.

The next morning Brian Scott and I accompanied him to hospital for the tests and there is no question that by this time he had become very nervous. After the tests were carried out we returned to Celtic Park via the city centre, where Darren was meeting his girlfriend Arlene for lunch. She was on standby to run him home after the meeting set up with the consultant neurosurgeon, Philip Barlow, in the afternoon. By that time he would have been able to analyse the results of the tests and give detailed advice.

The consultation with Mr Barlow duly took place that afternoon. I had asked Darren if he would prefer to see him alone or if he would like to be accompanied by Brian and me so that we could assist in asking any relevant questions and also hear first hand the information provided. He wanted us with him.

The message to Darren was clear. He was suffering from hydro-cephalus, commonly known as water on the brain. In that condition it was unthinkable for him to contemplate playing football again. He had a very straightforward choice. He either ended his playing career and led a normal life without taking any action in respect of his condition or he underwent laser brain surgery which, if carried out successfully, could give him a chance of continuing his playing career. Obviously, any surgery, particularly brain surgery, carried intrinsic risks which had to be weighed up very carefully indeed.

Darren was devastated. He had been as fit as a fiddle throughout his life. It had been explained that the condition from which he was suffering probably existed from birth but had only now come to light. A huge decision had to be taken. In the waiting-room outside Mr Barlow's consulting-room, Darren sat with Arlene, Brian and me as he attempted to come to terms with the situation. His immediate reaction was that he would have to face the surgery.

I put clearly to him what I considered to be the club's position. The decision had to be his, and entirely his. No pressure of any kind would be applied by the club and no thought should be given by him to the club's position. His contract would be honoured in full for the entire three-year period regardless of whether or not he ever kicked a ball again. His only consideration must be what was right for him and his family. The position presented to Darren in this respect was completely endorsed by Fergus McCann and the directors.

I insisted that Darren should not make a decision until he had had the opportunity to speak to his family at home and reflect on matters carefully overnight. Mr Barlow had made it clear that if he decided to go for the surgery, he should do so without delay.

Arlene was a superb calming influence. Darren conducted himself with great dignity. There was no trace of self-pity, simply a realisation that he was now facing a predicament which far exceeded the normal considerations of a football career. My admiration for the maturity he displayed was total.

I really did not have much doubt about the decision he would reach but it was imperative that he should consider the matter carefully in the bosom of his family, knowing that he would have total support from Celtic, whatever decision he reached. The next morning he confirmed that he had consulted with his parents, his sister and brother-in-law, and Arlene in great depth and was in no doubt that the correct option was surgery as soon as possible. Four days later I attended hospital with him as he checked in. Once again his general demeanour did him the utmost credit. He was nervous, all right, but completely focused on what he believed had to be done.

One of the most moving moments of my life, and certainly the most moving of my time at Celtic, was being present in the corner of the room behind Darren's family when he came round after the operation, recognised his loved ones and realised that the operation had been a success. My presence had been on the invitation of the family and for that I shall always be grateful. Darren later sent me a card with a bottle of champagne which he explained had to be opened only when he scored his first goal for the first team on his comeback. Three months later he scored a splendid goal at Pittodrie to help secure victory against Aberdeen and I forgot all sense of decorum, leaping from my seat to acclaim the moment. The champagne was quaffed the following day.

Sadly for Darren, this did not spark off the career he wanted at Celtic. There is a very unfortunate trend within Celtic Park for certain players to take much more than their fair share of abuse. After a brief honeymoon period following the brain surgery, Darren quickly fell into that category.

Frequently it is the most wholehearted of players who become victims. I recall Peter Grant, who was a committed Celtic man, coming in for that kind of abuse late in his career. Remarkably, Tom Boyd has also suffered, despite, in my opinion, having been one of the club's best servants for several seasons. David Hannah, another committed, wholehearted player, incurred the wrath of a section of the Celtic support before his return to Dundee United, as did Simon Donnelly, despite the fact that both of these young players made a significant contribution.

However, I think Darren found the change from being the star man at a smaller club to being a first-team squad player surrounded by top-class internationals very difficult to handle. As I have indicated, he tends to be a worrier and appears frequently to harbour feelings of insecurity. What he always needed at Celtic was a very long run as a first-choice player to enable him to win over the crowd. Under Wim Jansen that did not happen. He was in and out of the team and frequently on the bench. The effect of that was that he seemed to try too hard when he came on for fifteen or twenty minutes at the end of a match in order to try to make enough of an impression to convert the fans and persuade the coach to put him in the next starting eleven.

He was clearly perplexed and hurt when he started being booed as he took the field and I realised that his chances of getting an even break from some sections of the support were slim when he came on in the UEFA Cup tie at Celtic Park against Vittoria Guimaraes in October 1998. His arrival was greeted very cruelly by a large percentage of the support and yet he never put a foot wrong from the moment he took the field to the moment he played the key pass to Henrik Larsson to enable the Swede to score the killer goal.

My feeling has always been that the only crime which justifies hostile crowd reaction is a player not giving a hundred per cent in terms of effort. That accusation could never be levelled against Darren, yet it reached the stage where he really could not be selected for a home match. When I recall the gleam in the eye and the excitement he demonstrated the day he signed for Celtic, I am immensely saddened that it did not turn out to be the source of joy which he certainly deserved.

CHAPTER 8

Bust-up at Training

The other area of the team which still caused Wim Jansen serious concern was central defence. Considerable time and effort was put into assessing central defenders at home and abroad with a view to establishing who might be a dominant character who could act as the linchpin of the defence, just as Billy McNeill had been for the Lisbon Lions, followed in much more recent times by men like Mick McCarthy, Paul Elliott and Tony Mowbray. Everyone who attempts to fulfil that role at Celtic is eventually compared with Billy McNeill so it was a very tough challenge for any newcomer.

The assessment of potential candidates resulted in a short leet of two, both foreign, and one of them playing for West Ham United. His name was Marc Rieper. He was the one I was eventually instructed to pursue as first choice but once again there were substantial difficulties in making the deal happen.

Rieper was due to be out of contract at the end of the season so, from West Ham United's point of view, if they were unable to keep him it was much better to try to do a deal early in the season and command a decent fee. With the usual multitude of agents involved, the asking price moved from a figure in excess of £2 million to significantly less because of his contractual position. In August I eventually managed to reach agreement with West Ham on a fee and obtained permission to talk to the player. I travelled down to London one Wednesday evening when West Ham were playing Tottenham Hotspur and Rieper was marking Les Ferdinand. I arranged to meet him with his agent in a hotel in the city after the match and we eventually got together at around midnight. The meeting broke up at 3 a.m. and during that three-hour period money was never mentioned. Marc's principal interest was in Celtic as a club, our ambitions and our plans for the future. He wanted to know all he could about the club, the coaching staff and the players, some of whom he knew from his international career with Denmark and from playing in the Premiership.

It was refreshing to deal with a man in the world of football whose agent never at any stage in that initial meeting said 'How much?'. His interest was in making certain that coming to Celtic was the correct career move and that the club was as ambitious as he was to win trophies and do well in Europe. My task was to sell the club effectively while at the same time completing my own research into the character of the individual we had targeted. I was completely satisfied in that respect and clearly he, too, was happy with what he heard about Celtic, because by the end of the evening it was established that, subject to terms and conditions being agreed with his agent, he was happy to come to Glasgow.

The next problem, however, was the fact that West Ham were unwilling to commit to a date for his release. They told me initially that because of injuries they needed to keep him for three more matches, and that number was later increased to the extent that it became a matter of some concern whether or not the deal would go ahead. But, being Glasgow, the wild-card factor was sure to apply. Stories began to appear in the newspapers to the effect that Rangers were on the brink of stepping in to buy him. Whether or not there was any truth in any of these stories I will never know. However, my confidence in the integrity of Rieper was such that I knew in my own mind that if there were any possibility of his being deflected from his resolve to come to Celtic, he or his agent would have told me. So when the press asked me repeatedly about this situation and in particular how I would react if we lost him to Rangers, I had to hold my nerve and continue with the policy of not talking about players registered to other clubs and not dealing with names about whom there was speculation.

Wim Jansen was clearly also being told all about the possibility of Rangers stepping in. He began to ask me for progress reports, which he seldom did. I explained to him the difficulty lay with West Ham's requirements and their reluctance to let him go while they still had injury problems. I asked him if he wanted to move to our second choice. He asked me directly if I believed the Rieper deal could be concluded. I replied that I was confident it would happen within a reasonably short space of time, although I could not guarantee the precise date. 'On that basis we'll hold on for Rieper,' he said. I must confess that I respected his handling of that situation and the faith that he appeared to be placing in me in terms of my judgement on whether or not the deal would come off, regardless of any allegations about Rangers' interest.

Sure enough, my faith in Rieper proved to be justified. I was able to agree terms with his agent as soon as West Ham agreed to his release and the deal was concluded some twenty-four hours before a difficult away match at Motherwell on 12 September. The whole process had lasted the best part of a month and shortly before the deal was concluded our second choice as central defender was transferred – talk about holding your nerve!

While I was greatly encouraged by Wim's handling of the Rieper situation and by the fact that he appeared to place some trust in me, I was surprised by his reaction to the Tosh McKinlay/Henrik Larsson training incident in November. Two days before we were due to play the first Old Firm match of the season at Ibrox, I was asked around lunchtime to go urgently to the coach's room because there had been an incident at Barrowfield in which it was alleged that Tosh McKinlay had headbutted Henrik Larsson during a training match and inflicted some damage on Henrik's face. The press knew all about it and it was set to become the major story of the day.

In the coach's room I established that Henrik had gone straight from training to the airport to return to Sweden for a family funeral, although that was interpreted in at least one newspaper as him running out on Celtic because of the training-ground incident. Tosh McKinlay had gone home. The message from Wim and Murdo was clear – this was my problem. Since they had been present at the time, I asked them for a description of what had happened and they told me that, for no apparent reason, and without provocation, Tosh had stepped away from the ball and headbutted Henrik.

As always at Celtic, there was a list of factors to consider and priorities to establish. The priority, without question, remained the match against Rangers two days later. Henrik was scheduled to fly back from Sweden in time for the match and Tosh was down to play for the reserves at Celtic Park.

I suggested to Wim and Murdo that in view of the fact that I could not speak to Henrik until after the match against Rangers, the main priority was to defuse the situation as much as possible prior to the match and avoid exacerbating the media circus. That, for me, meant telling Tosh to stay away from training the following day and not to report for the reserve match on the Saturday. They agreed. I telephoned Tosh at home that afternoon and told him what I had agreed with Wim and Murdo, namely that he should not report for training on the

Friday or for the match at Celtic Park on the Saturday. I made it clear to him that this was in no way disciplinary action because the matter had still not been investigated properly but was simply a precaution to take the sting out of the situation as far as the media were concerned. He readily understood.

There was an international match the following midweek and Tosh was in the Scotland squad. I suggested to him that he should stay away from the club until he reported for Scotland duty and concentrate on the international match. We would deal with the matter the following Thursday morning when the dust had settled. There was no suggestion of any suspension being imposed or disciplinary action being taken. The decisions which had been made had been made in the best interests of the club's prospects for the match against Rangers. Everything else had to be shelved in the meantime.

You can therefore imagine my anger when Hugh Keevins of the *Sunday Mail* wrote that weekend about Tosh having been judged and sentenced by being suspended from Celtic Park. To say Tosh was displeased with the article was an understatement. I have known Hugh Keevins for the best part of thirty years. We originally worked together at D.C. Thomson & Co. Ltd, the publishers of the *Sunday Post* and *Weekly News*. He was a good guy. We remained in contact as his journalistic career blossomed and he moved on to *The Scotsman* and Radio Clyde. He was still a good guy. I carried out legal work for him during that time and enjoyed an excellent relationship.

But during Hugh's career, the world of sports journalism has changed markedly. Thirty years ago you had to have reliable sources, preferably quotable, for any story. Facts had to be checked and verified. You were answerable to sports editors for the accuracy of your material.

I have already mentioned the pressure now on journalists to produce 'exclusives'. While it applies principally at the tabloid end of the market, the broadsheets nowadays are not immune. If a reporter comes up with an inaccurate 'exclusive', he or she can gather more copy when the material is denied the next day. You will never read 'We got it wrong'. So checking facts in advance of printing is frequently dangerous, because you may find your story doesn't add up.

As a result, Hugh joined the hysteria about the identity of the new head coach at Celtic prior to Wim Jansen's appointment. He was the man who announced through the pages of *The Scotsman* the day before Wim Jansen's appointment that Artur Jorge would be the new Celtic head coach.

When he moved to the *Sunday Mail* I was astonished. I mentioned this to him on one of his visits to Celtic Park in the summer of 1997 and he assured me that his role at the *Sunday Mail* was to be 'Captain Sensible'. He would not be sucked into any tabloid morass which had resulted from the circulation wars. He had negotiated a contract whereby if he lost his job by adhering to his principles and coming into conflict with his masters, he would be handsomely remunerated. I listened and indicated I would give him six weeks before he fell into line to satisfy his masters. I take no pleasure whatsoever in having been proved correct.

This was adequately demonstrated in his coverage of the Tosh McKinlay situation. What was written was palpable nonsense and I regret that I felt compelled to tell him so at Celtic Park the following Saturday. I told him in no uncertain terms what I thought of his previous Sunday's article, not knowing that Tosh McKinlay was accepting the opportunity similarly to denounce him on Radio Clyde! That gave Hugh a basis for writing another snarling article about the manner in which I had approached him, pointing out how much I had changed during my time at Celtic. No doubt there was some truth in that, because no one stays the same while undergoing a series of new experiences. The problem is, that applies to him too. Sadly he has followed the *Sunday Mail* line of attacking Celtic at virtually every turn and writing endless columns of negativity, much of which is based on his misconceptions, with lots of misinformation.

The investigation into the training-ground incident continued after the match at Ibrox that Saturday, which was lost by one goal to nil. I spoke to Henrik Larsson and obtained his version of events on the Thursday. He explained the situation in a very calm and even manner with no hint of exaggeration or attempt to heighten trouble for Tosh. Indeed, he tried to keep the whole affair in context and to minimise the seriousness of it all. His approach reflected enormous credit on him.

Armed with the eye-witness reports from Wim Jansen and Murdo MacLeod and the evidence from Henrik Larsson, it remained only for me to speak to Tosh on his return from international duty. There was no doubt he appeared the guilty party. I reported to Wim and Murdo that my intention was to speak to Tosh prior to his reporting for training on Thursday morning. I advised them of Henrik's evidence and invited suggestions from them on the appropriate course of action, subject to anything Tosh had to say. Murdo asked me what options were open to us. I explained that we could do anything from giving him a warning to terminating his contract for serious misconduct. Murdo thought we should sack him. Wim didn't demur.

I asked Murdo if his attitude would be exactly the same if Henrik had been the guilty party and had headbutted Tosh. 'Oh, that would be entirely different,' he replied. He couldn't explain to me why it would be different. I suggested to him that I was not very keen on his idea of justice. Justice could not be served by assessing the immediate value to the team of one player against another, but only by a fair assessment of all the facts and circumstances which would apply to any player, right across the board. The effect was that it was up to me. Wim and Murdo appeared to want no more to do with the whole situation.

At 8.30 a.m. on the Thursday after the international match, I telephoned Tosh at home and suggested that rather than report for training that morning he should wait in the house and I would visit him to discuss the training-ground incident. He readily agreed. I arrived at his house at about 9.30 a.m. and asked for his version of events. He immediately responded that he had been out of order. He took full responsibility for the incident and explained that he had formed the view in a split second that Henrik was attacking him and reacted with the headbutt. He now realised that the reaction to Henrik had been wrong and sought to apportion blame to no one except himself.

I explained that I had spoken in detail to Henrik and to Wim and Murdo and, together with the version of events he had just given me, it was clear that he was entirely the guilty party – which left me to decide on the appropriate disciplinary action. He accepted that. I then advised him that it was my intention to fine him and that he would have fourteen days from intimation in writing of the fine to lodge any appeal. I told him how much the fine would be. He indicated immediately that there would be no question of any appeal. He felt he had been given a fair hearing and said that he had no complaint with the disciplinary action being taken. He had been out of order and knew he had to pay the penalty. 'I thought you were going to sack me,' he said. 'I thought it would suit certain people to get me out of the club.'

I was troubled that he should have thought that was likely. He clearly had formed the impression that he was not looked upon as a valuable and important player in the squad. Notwithstanding a fine performance at Anfield against Liverpool, he had scarcely seen the light of day since as far as first-team duty was concerned.

I suppose headbutting someone perceived as a star player very much favoured in the eyes of the head coach would have given anyone substantial cause for concern. But the fine did not end Tosh's obligations within the club. He still had to square things with Henrik and with the rest of his team-mates in the dressing-room. I was delighted to learn that he called Henrik that Thursday afternoon, went round to see him, cleared the air and resolved matters between them.

The following morning he asked Tom Boyd to bring the players to the dressing-room before training, where he offered a blanket apology to everyone for the disruption he had caused – before being swamped by the usual volume of stick which meant that he was welcome back in the fold.

It was a nasty incident, and one which should never have happened, but it did eventually serve to demonstrate the high calibre of the two individuals involved, Henrik Larsson and Tosh McKinlay. Tosh's handling of being effectively ostracised from that point on as a first-team player did him enormous credit and I was overjoyed for him when he realised his ambition of playing in the World Cup finals in France despite his lack of first-team football throughout the season.

CHAPTER 9

David Hay's Demise

David Hay really broke my heart. I couldn't have been happier to find him at the club when I arrived and I believed that he would be a staunch ally and support to me, especially in the difficult settling-in period.

All the early signs were good. He could not have been more helpful to me in those early days. His general knowledge of the club and the way it operated was invaluable. There were sensitivities, though. He had applied for the job I had been given and, indeed, had been operating as acting manager since the departure of Tommy Burns with effect from 1 June 1997. I had been made aware by the club of the agreement with David to the effect that he would operate as acting manager until the new management structure was put in place and he would have an enhanced salary to reflect that responsibility until 31 July 1997. He had also been promised an extension of one year to his existing fixed-term contract which was due to expire on 30 June 1997, although the capacity in which he would operate would not be established until the new management structure was in place.

We had known each other for years and as his solicitor I had negotiated his severance package when his contract as manager with Celtic was terminated in 1987. It was obviously a matter of great concern to me that he should think that I had to have him in the management team for at least a year in order to honour the agreement reached with the board. But I was most anxious to ensure that he knew that he was very much wanted at the club and that I was not accepting him on sufferance because of a previous arrangement.

It was on that basis that the decision was reached to appoint him as assistant general manager in addition to his duties as chief scout. David appeared to be delighted at this recognition and the tangible confirmation of his importance to the organisation. The usual press announcement was made and a potentially sensitive situation appeared to have been satisfactorily resolved.

A few days after the announcement of his appointment, he approached me and suggested that his salary should be increased. I indicated to him that because I had just arrived at the club and had had no previous direct dealings with him on contractual matters, I thought it more appropriate that he should discuss this aspect of his employment with Eric Riley, the financial director and the director in charge of personnel. I cleared with Eric his willingness to deal with David and withdrew from any further discussions on this subject. The view I took was that if David and I were to work closely together, it would be better if we were not directly negotiating with each other over remuneration.

David then advised me that he had reflected further on the matter and thought it would be better if his brother Brian, an accountant, dealt directly with Eric Riley. I offered no objection and then learned from Eric that a meeting had taken place at which he had offered a small increase in David's original salary and an enhanced executive bonus scheme, but had been told by Brian that this was unacceptable. He clearly had much greater aspirations in terms of remuneration than Eric had demonstrated. Eric explained to me that he had tried to clarify to Brian why he felt the offer made was fair but indicated that Brian was not happy with the proposal.

I was then approached by David, who was clearly very upset about the offer made by Eric to his brother. He told me that he felt both he and Brian had been insulted by the offer made and he felt so badly about how he understood the meeting had been conducted that he believed he would have to leave the club. He was clearly very agitated. It later emerged that for some reason his brother had apparently not reported to him the bonus-scheme offer.

I tried very hard to calm him down and invited him to reflect carefully on matters before jumping to any conclusion of that kind because jobs in football at the salary he was receiving were few and far between. I also told him that I was very anxious that he should stay. I managed to placate him and persuaded him to take at least a day or two to reflect on things.

The next time I spoke to him about the matter he was much calmer but indicated he was still thoroughly aggrieved and was considering his position very carefully. He still felt so insulted that he feared he would have to quit. Once again I tried to placate him. He asked me to see what I could do by intervening and talking to the board, and Eric Riley in particular. I did try to explain to him my difficulty in this respect since Eric Riley was a director and the board was fully aware of the overall situation. We had also agreed at the outset that he and I would not deal directly on this issue.

While I did speak to Eric Riley, there was nothing constructive I could say to David and I hoped very much that he would calm down and that the issue would fade away. On two or three occasions, however, during the following month or so, David asked me if I had done anything about 'his situation'. I always indicated that I had not done anything because that was the correct position. Eventually, he asked if I had any objection to him going direct to Fergus McCann on the subject and I made it clear that I did not have any such objection if he felt that was necessary.

Some time later he came back to me and said that he had gone to see Fergus, who had listened to him but then referred him back to me as his immediate line manager. I then discussed the matter with Eric Riley on a more formal basis. I had certainly spoken to him informally on a number of occasions in the past, indicating to him that David was very unhappy with the outcome of the meeting with his brother. Now I suggested to Eric that in place of the discretionary bonus system which had been in place before or the company executive bonus scheme which had been proposed by Eric to Brian, I could perhaps put together a specific bonus scheme linked to David's precise role at the club in the hope that this might resolve the problem. Eric agreed that I could attempt this.

I then told David that he had to accept the fact that the salary would not change but I was prepared to attempt to negotiate a fresh bonus scheme. I asked him if he wanted a bonus scheme based on his recruitment of players and their value to the club. I was conscious of the fact that he had been involved in the recruitment of players in the recent past who had been sold on for substantial profits and I wondered if he wanted a bonus scheme based on such a proposition.

He indicated that he wanted a bonus scheme linked to the winning of trophies only. He thought that was what we were all aiming for at the club and that he should be rewarded in the event that trophies were won. He took the very responsible view that it was his job to find and recruit the correct players for the club, and if he did that then trophies would be won and he could then be rewarded.

I then devised a new bonus scheme which was approved by the board in which he would receive a specific bonus if the club won the league championship, the Scottish Cup or the Coca-Cola Cup. I put my proposal to David and he agreed that the figures were reasonable. He then came back to me and asked if I could arrange for him to receive a proportion of the first-team players' match bonus. He suggested that a figure of roughly two thirds of the players' bonuses on a match basis would be appropriate. If I agreed to that, together with trophy bonuses and the basic salary, then he would be happy.

I reflected on this and discussed it with the directors. Like me, they could see no basis at all for adding players' bonuses to the package. David had explained to me that he believed if he was given the players' bonus as well, he would then be receiving the salary he ought to have received in the first place. The decision was taken to reject his proposal.

It was my task to communicate the decision to him and explain that there would be no possibility of players' match bonuses being added to the package. I explained that he was really attempting to obtain his rate of salary by another means and the club had already fixed a value on his responsibilities. He was not happy.

From about mid-September David largely withdrew from using the office which he shared with me. I formed the impression that he was in some peculiar way working to rule. That point was put to him. He confirmed that he was very unhappy about the deal on offer and was still considering his position. Every time this was raised I tried to persuade him to stay on board and I continually advised him that I was anxious to sit down and plan a more orchestrated system for scouting networks and for continuing the business for which we had been engaged. He showed no interest in talking about that in any detail at all. He kept on saying that he would simply continue to do the job in the meantime but consider his position generally.

However, in terms of his job description as assistant general manager, there was really no attempt of any kind to cover his responsibilities or enter into any kind of dialogue. He withdrew more and more and a pattern evolved whereby he seldom appeared at his desk except at around 4 p.m., when he came to collect messages or mail, having spent his time elsewhere at Celtic Park. The situation was extremely uncomfortable. With hindsight, I probably allowed things to drift on much too long, since I did feel somewhat inhibited by his earlier contractual discussions with the club and the obligation to keep him in employment until June 1998.

Over the course of this period David spent his working day in the main, I believe, in the coach's room with Wim Jansen and Murdo MacLeod. There is no question that they had become extremely close. I had quickly become aware of being distanced from the technical football staff, partly because of the geography of the office layout and partly because of the fact that these three were constantly together and I was not spending a great deal of time with them.

Accordingly, over the period of September and October I made a concerted effort to change this by ensuring that I spent part of every day with them, and I formed the view, rightly or wrongly, that substantial progress was being made in enhancing the overall relationships among the four. However, David continually made references to his dissatisfaction with his lot. On two separate occasions he indicated to me that he would tell me in a few days' time whether he wanted to stay or leave. Eventually, he began discussing the possibility of leaving if he could receive 'a package'.

On several occasions I told him that I could not understand why the Eric Riley/Brian Hay meeting had affected him so badly and why he could not put this behind him and simply carry on with the job. He did admit to me on more than one occasion that this meeting gnawed away at him constantly and he could not get it completely out of his mind. He also admitted that it had affected his enthusiasm for his work and that while he still believed that he was doing the job properly, some of the heart had been knocked out of him.

Several conversations in this vein took place over a lengthy period of time and on each occasion I tried to persuade David to forget that background and to continue working, since things were beginning to go well for the club on the field and, therefore, off the field. I did become a little concerned when he said from time to time, 'I think you will win the league.' I could not understand why it was not 'we will win the league'.

The entire matter was becoming one of substantial embarrassment for me in that people were constantly asking me where David was and I could seldom tell them. Everyone in the office knew that he virtually never used his desk or appeared at his workstation. Eventually, at the end of October, I raised the matter again and said that it had to be resolved. I had to have a clear indication of willingness to continue in a proper manner or be told that he wished to leave. By this time I must confess that I had decided to stop trying to persuade him to stay since I had been doing this to no avail.

Eventually, on Monday, 27 October 1997, David told me that he had decided to leave on the condition that he received a satisfactory pay-off. I did not try to persuade him to stay. I did say to him that I thought there would be substantial difficulty in persuading the board to allow him to leave and at the same time give him a pay-off when the club position was that we wanted him to stay and work. I made it clear that any employee was entitled to withdraw his labour and cease receiving salary but it was really impossible to suggest that the desire to go was subject only to a pay-off, otherwise things would continue as before. I indicated to him that I considered that position to be untenable.

Nevertheless, I undertook to investigate the possibility of a pay-off. I discussed the matter with the directors and it was agreed that we would accept his resignation and make a payment of compensation. The board had agreed to the pay-off.

On the evening of Wednesday, 29 October, I put this to David. I made reference to the money with a fairly detailed analysis of what considerations had been taken on board in arriving at the sum concerned, but when I eventually told him the amount he flared up and demonstrated at least a partial loss of temper, saying that the proposal was 'an insult'. He indicated that there was no way in which this was acceptable and while he did not expect an offer which would be acceptable, he did not expect one as low as that.

I asked him what he intended to do and he said that he would continue working with Wim Jansen from the coach's room as he had been doing for the previous weeks. I told him that this was unacceptable. He responded by saying that the club should then decide what they wanted to do about it. This was undoubtedly a show of defiance, if not bravado.

I then counselled him that his reaction was not sensible and that there was a distinct possibility that the club would take action.

This could mean him leaving the club with no money at all. He remained totally defiant. I told him he had rendered the whole work-ing situation untenable by his attitude. I said that the board would have to consider the matter in the light of his reaction and I was concerned that there was a distinct possibility of the contract being terminated.

He then told me that I should ask Wim Jansen what he thought. I asked him what this had to do with Wim Jansen and what Wim knew about the situation. He explained that he had told Wim that he had contractual difficulties and was not happy with his remuneration but he had given him no details. I told him that I thought it was unfair and inappropriate to involve Wim but he was adamant that he had simply intimated the general position without giving any detail.

I interpreted the reference to Wim as some kind of threat that, should the club decide to take serious action, David felt he could depend on Wim to be an ally.

With a very heavy heart I reflected on the matter overnight and reported to the board on Thursday, 30 October. Having given my report on the current state of play, I was asked for my recommendation on the correct course of action. I said that I could see no other solution than to terminate the contract because I felt David had struck at the very heart of the essential relationship between employer and employee and had created an untenable working situation. It was clear that he was not prepared to work as assistant general manager or be party to any discussions about how the scouting operation could be set up better, quite apart from other matters which I had constantly mentioned to him over many weeks.

However, I also recommended that we should still make a compensation payment to him. This, I felt, would reflect a substantial degree of sympathy for David's position following his failure to obtain the original general manager's job which I was now performing and would reflect his past service to the club. I also believed that in these circumstances the club would not only be acting fairly but would be seen to be acting fairly. This was certainly everyone's wish.

These recommendations to terminate the contract and make the payment were approved by the board. There was obviously delicacy relating to the Wim Jansen position and I indicated to the board that it was appropriate for me to speak to him in advance to alert him to the overall position without giving any details or offering any real criticism of David.

On the afternoon of Thursday, 30 October, I did discuss the matter with Wim Jansen. He voiced his dissatisfaction with any difficulty relating to David's position. He saw him as a very important asset and one he wanted to keep on board. That was exactly my position, too, but I informed Wim that David had made the position untenable. Wim indicated that his interpretation of the matter was that it was about money and nothing else, and his suggestion was that we should simply pay David whatever it took to keep him on board. I gave the honest and sincere view that this was no longer simply about money but had taken on more complex proportions, although I was not able to advise him of the precise basis for the situation we now found ourselves in.

During that day David had operated as though nothing had happened the previous night. He was in the players' lounge with Wim Jansen, Murdo MacLeod and others and appeared to be in very good form. He certainly made no attempt to try to speak to me on a one-to-one basis. Eventually, at around 5 p.m., he arrived at our office and I asked him if he had had any change of heart since the previous evening. Had he at that stage indicated that he had reflected on the matter and formed the view that he had made a misjudgement, I would certainly have been prepared to listen. However, he was absolutely clear, and slightly belligerent, in saying that his position had not changed in any way.

At that point I told him that in these circumstances I had no option but to terminate his contract and sign the letter which I had prepared setting out the basis for this. I told him he would still receive a cheque for the sum which had been discussed the previous evening but he immediately replied that he would not take it. I explained that the cheque was being offered unconditionally and there was therefore no reason why he should not accept it. I tried to hand him the termination letter with the cheque but he refused to accept this and insisted that he wanted to have reasons in writing for his dismissal. I told him that I was prepared to provide such reasons in writing and would do so the following day. He then indicated that he would return the following day to collect his belongings and my correspondence. I tried to tell him that the initial letter could be taken in isolation, separately from the letter with the reasons for his dismissal, but he still would not take anything from me and said he would see me the following morning.

The next day he did not come to see me. I was advised that he had arrived in the building and was in the players' area. I had prepared the letter outlining the reasons for the termination of his contract and kept waiting for him to arrive to collect it. He did not show up. Early in the afternoon I attended the normal Friday press conference with Wim Jansen, but before that I advised him of the state of play. He expressed his anger at the termination and told me that he was very unhappy indeed about the situation. I tried to explain to him that David had made the situation impossible. He did not appear to want to listen.

After the press conference Wim went to watch a youth match at Barrowfield and I was then made aware of the fact that David had also gone to that match and had later returned to Celtic Park with Wim and Murdo MacLeod. By that time I was attending a management meeting which was interrupted by a message that David Hay was asking to see me. The request appeared to be for me to go down to the coach's room to see him, which would mean a discussion in the presence of Wim and Murdo. I was not prepared to be involved in that kind of four-way debate.

I sent a message back to the effect that I could see him in ten minutes if he cared to come to our office. When that was conveyed to him he indicated to my secretary on the telephone that Wim and Murdo had gone, as though that had some bearing on whether or not we should meet. He said that he would call my secretary back and he eventually did so to say that he had to leave immediately but would report for work as normal on Monday and would see me then. This appeared very strange.

At precisely that time we were heavily involved in trying to bring a new striker to the club. The relentless clamour from supporters for a striker, fuelled by the media, was ongoing. We were very conscious of the fact that with Darren Jackson and Tommy Johnson unfit we were in serious trouble if anything happened to Henrik Larsson or Simon Donnelly.

David had gone to substantial trouble to identify a suitable striker. Eventually, he gave Harald Brattbakk his recommendation in customary fashion: 'He's no' bad, he'll get you goals.' The difficulty was that his club, Rosenborg, champions of Norway, were still actively involved in the Champions' League. When I made contact with them about Brattbakk's availability I was told that they would not consider any sale until after the final Champions' League match on 10 December 1997. This was much longer than Celtic wanted to wait but there appeared to be no viable alternative and accordingly a decision was taken to pursue the possibility of bringing Harald to Celtic.

Rosenborg gave permission for Harald to come to Glasgow with his agent to have a look around and to discuss personal terms. Harald's agent was a man called Erik Soler who had been a player at the time David Hay was coach at Lillestrom. Accordingly, David had made the arrangements with the agent for the visit to Glasgow, which was due to take place the same evening David was due to clear his desk and leave his employment at Celtic.

Harald and his agent were arriving at Glasgow Airport late on the Friday evening and I had arranged to go to their hotel at 9 a.m. on the Saturday to give them a tour of Celtic Park and the city. When I arrived at the appointed hour, the doorman told me that David had been at the hotel the previous evening.

That particular Saturday, Celtic were playing Dunfermline at East End Park. After spending the morning with Harald and Erik Soler, I left them at the hotel at lunchtime and indicated that I would return after the match to discuss personal terms. I arrived at the hotel at about 7 p.m. and spent the evening negotiating Harald's contract. The meeting was concluded with handshakes reflecting agreement all round and I left at about 9.35 p.m. As I walked out of the hotel through the reception area, I saw David at the reception desk on the internal phone.

On the morning of Monday, 3 November, I waited again for David to arrive. There was no sign of him. I then learned that he had arrived in the players' area and I sent a message asking him to come and see me. I received a return message to the effect that he was seeing a couple of players and would see me later.

Eventually, at around 1.30 p.m., he arrived in our office. I asked him what he was doing, bearing in mind the termination of his contract on Thursday evening. He said that he would like to bring his brother Brian into the meeting 'as a witness'. I offered no objection. He then told me that as far as he was concerned his contract had not been terminated because he had received nothing in writing. I explained to him that the two letters which he had refused to accept on Thursday and Friday had been posted to him by first-class mail and should be at his home. The settlement cheque was enclosed. He indicated that he had left home that morning before the mail had arrived but that he had received nothing on Saturday morning. He accepted my offer to provide him with copies of the letters and read them before folding them up and putting them in his pocket. He indicated to Brian that he would show him the letters later.

The whole meeting was calm and amicable apart from the fact that David was clearly slightly agitated. Brian replied that there was no point in them staying since the situation was now perfectly clear and he suggested that he and David should leave. David indicated that he wanted to take his belongings but then realised that there was quite a volume to take away and asked if he could come back later in the afternoon to do so. Obviously, I had no objection. The two men then left.

At about 6.45 p.m. David reappeared in the office to collect his belongings. I was still there, in the company of David Kells, the commercial director. There was no aggravation or animosity and we left him to go about the business of taking away his personal belongings.

The reference to seeking reasons for dismissal in writing alerted me to the fact that David had taken legal advice. Accordingly, I anticipated the possibility of an industrial tribunal application, although I did not believe that the club would have anything to fear.

CHAPTER 10

The Tribunal Decides

Wim Jansen was not a happy man. He made one of his very unusual sorties to the East End administration offices the following day to express his anger at the David Hay situation to Fergus McCann. He made his feelings clear to me too during that week. The principal difficulty I had with this was that I had taken a clear decision not to go into detail about the whole saga relating to David with Wim for two reasons. First, it was not likely to have any beneficial effect, and second, David and Wim clearly had become very close friends. In these circumstances, I had no wish whatsoever to say anything bad about David or to enter into a debate.

I was well aware of the fact that David was in constant touch with Wim and Murdo during the days immediately following his departure from the club. Clearly David had given Wim his version of events and there was simply no point whatsoever in my trying to persuade Wim that the club's position was justified, especially when he had been so angry and volatile whenever the issue had been mentioned.

I was conscious also of the fact that during the initial discussion about David Hay's dissatisfaction Wim had indicated to me that Murdo was also unhappy. When I asked him to clarify the situation he simply said he wasn't happy about his contract and he did not think he was being paid well enough. Clearly David and Murdo were seeking to enlist the help of the man they believed held the power in order to improve their own positions. My perception was then and has always remained that poor Wim was being used but didn't appreciate the fact.

While I fully expected the industrial tribunal application to proceed, I was seriously disappointed and shocked when David sold his story to the *Sunday Mail*. He tried to justify it by stating that he had to speak out because 'they said I was on the take'.

The newspaper articles do not stand close scrutiny. At no time have I ever suggested that David Hay was on 'the take' or involved in anything corrupt. There was no whisper of any such skulduggery in my hearing among any of those in power at Celtic. However, I can confirm that various journalists had asked if Davie had gone because he was on the fiddle. In his first article in the *Sunday Mail* he complained about how difficult it was to take when 'you are falsely branded like this by cowardly, faceless rumourmongers'. I can assure Davie that the people who appeared to upset him were certainly not anyone I knew within Celtic Park.

The message Davie tried to convey was that I forced him out. He also allowed the newspaper to pursue the sinister angle about Celtic men being driven away from the club. 'It seems that the new Parkhead regime no longer want traditional Celtic men at the club,' Davie's article continued, under the banner 'The Truth'.

Sadly, the relationship between the truth and what appeared in his various articles was difficult to establish. Davie was able to confirm that when he was cross-examined at the industrial tribunal which took place in May and June of 1998. Having given detailed evidence which contradicted many elements of the *Sunday Mail* story 'The Truth', Davie was asked to reconcile what he had now said under oath with what had appeared in the newspaper, since the two did not match. Approximately seven items of complete contradiction were pointed out to him, and Davie actually said within the tribunal proceedings, 'That's the papers, you know what they are like.'

He was asked if he had approved the material which had appeared in the *Sunday Mail*. He said that copies had been sent to him to proofread but he hadn't bothered because he knew the paper would not take any notice anyway. 'Jock has taken four months to dismantle 110 years of our tradition,' ranted Davie in a further attempt to justify his £15,000 fee from the paper. Perhaps that also justified introducing the sinister religious connotation which appeared in the articles. He alleged that he said to me, 'You don't want me here, do you? If you are going to get rid of me you'd better do it right.' What absolute fiction. Mind you, many areas of fiction were picked up clearly at the industrial tribunal and Davie seemed totally unperturbed by it all.

It's not pleasant or easy to read such nonsense appearing in a newspaper, although when Davie confessed at the industrial tribunal that much of it was nonsense I almost became angry with him for the first time. You see, I could never feel angry with Davie. I have always liked him and I still like him. I think he was very badly influenced by anonymous people and totally misjudged the overall situation at the club when he campaigned for more money. Yet when we met in the gents between sessions at the tribunal office, our discussion could scarcely have been more cordial.

The particular sadness I retain is because I went out of my way not to communicate the details of the reasons for Davie's departure for so long. Indeed, but for the industrial tribunal application, I would still not be talking about it now. At the time he left, I simply indicated via the *Celtic View* that Davie had left the club and that we wished him well. I left it to him to make all the running in terms of the public view of the matter and I was determined to adhere to the privacy of the situation even though I was continually pressed for answers by journalists and by supporters at club events.

The first time I spoke out in detail about the whole situation was at the industrial tribunal hearing when I gave evidence. The coverage of that was interesting. The fact that a hearing was taking place made big news on radio and television and in the newspapers. There was substantial coverage of the evidence with the packaging regularly appearing to me to be balanced in favour of the individual applicant. When the industrial tribunal issued its judgement there were some reports but it was clearly not the result which many elements of the tabloid press appeared to want. Very little of the written decision extending to eighteen pages ever saw the light of day in the press.

The date of the judgement was 1 July 1998, at which time I was being constantly pilloried for the fact that Celtic still had not appointed a new head coach to replace Wim Jansen. I suppose the chances of details of the reasons for the tribunal's decision being well publicised then were remote.

The unanimous decision of the tribunal was that Davie had not been unfairly dismissed and that his complaint of breach of contract should be refused.

The tribunal reported its view of the two versions of events from June 1997 to October 1997 as provided by me and by David. They said, *inter alia*:

> The Tribunal preferred the version of events given by Mr Brown. The reasons for this are as follows:
>
> 1. *The Tribunal's view of Mr Brown's evidence*
> The Tribunal were impressed by Mr Brown as a witness. They believed him when he said that he had known the applicant for a long time and had a considerable liking and respect for Mr Hay.
>
> He was not certain about dates of various meetings but it was

accepted by the Tribunal that the negotiations were conducted on a very informal basis since both men had known each other for a considerable period of time. Mr Brown's version of events especially in the vital period from 27 October to 3 November was given in a very frank and candid way. He did not hesitate to say that Mr Hay was extremely angry on the 29 October and that the relationship had deteriorated by that time.

The Tribunal also believe that prior to 29 October he said to Mr Hay that, even if he was determined to leave, he shouldn't jump too quickly and should take his time and look around for a job. This appears to the Tribunal to be only sensible. The Tribunal accepted Mr Brown as a credible and reliable witness. However, there are another four factors which the Tribunal consider lent credence to the evidence of Mr Brown. They are points 2 to 5 which follow:

2. The evidence of Mr Reilly (sic)

The evidence of Mr Reilly confirmed the evidence of Mr Brown in relation to the vital period from 27 October to 30 October. He confirmed that Mr Brown had reported to the Board that there had been a meeting on 27 October during which Mr Hay had requested to leave the club with a pay-off. Mr Reilly also confirmed Mr Brown's version of the meeting on 29 October. He said that Mr Brown reported to the board that Mr Hay wanted a figure of £50,000. It was noticeable that Mr Hay did not say at any point in his evidence that he had mentioned the figure of £50,000 with a £30,000 tax-free element.

3. The period from 27 October to 29 October

On Mr Brown's version of events Mr Hay intimated on 27 October that he wanted to leave with a pay-off. On 29 October Mr Brown then approached Mr Hay with a figure of £16,500 as a pay-off. This sits logically.

On Mr Hay's version of events on 27 October Mr Hay said to Mr Brown that he thought that Mr Brown wanted him to leave. Mr Brown denied this but Mr Hay said to him that if he did want him to leave then Celtic would have to honour the contract.

On the 29th, according to Mr Hay's version, Mr Brown came to him and made him an offer of £16,500 to leave the club. But in Mr Hay's version Mr Brown had said two days previously that he did not want him to leave. The Tribunal took the view that it was more likely that the 'Brown version' is correct.

4. Mr Hay's actions after 29 October

On Mr Brown's version, Mr Hay intimated on 29 October that he would simply work on, would not go near Mr Brown and would continue working in the coach's room. This is exactly what Mr Hay did.

Mr Hay, when giving evidence, had difficulty in explaining why he came into work on Friday 31st, after being advised that he had been dismissed from the club on the 30th. His only explanation was that he thought Celtic might change their mind. However, if Mr Hay was to be believed that the dismissal had come completely out of the blue in the midst of negotiations then one would have thought that he would have been complaining either to Brown or more likely to someone in a more senior position, for example, Mr McCann, that he was being treated unfairly. However, he made no attempt to see Mr Reilly or Mr McCann but only attempted to see Mr Brown on the Friday evening at 4.40 p.m. When advised that Mr Brown was engaged, Mr Hay said that he had a meeting elsewhere and could not wait to see him. The Tribunal considered that this was not the type of behaviour that one would have expected from an employee whose dismissal came as a shock to him whilst he was merely negotiating terms of employment.

5. The letter to Mr Hay dated 31 October 1997

In the letter dated 31 October 1997 to Mr Hay giving reasons for his dismissal, Mr Brown writes as follows:

'A combination of the clear expression of your wish to leave, subject to receiving a satisfactory pay-off, and the defiant manner in which you made it clear that you would continue operating independently as before, struck at the heart of the essential relationship between employer and employee, and created a working situation which was wholly untenable.'

This is consistent with Mr Brown's evidence.

Mr Hay received this letter on 3 November and did not object to the facts contained therein by appealing as he had a right to in the terms of his contract or by having his solicitor write immediately, intimating that the facts contained in the letter were wrong.

For all these reasons, the Tribunal preferred the version of events given by Mr Brown. We believe that Mr Hay intimated to Mr Brown on two or three occasions during the September/October period that he wanted to leave the club and accept that

Mr Hay said on 27 October he had made a final decision that he wanted to leave but he wanted a pay-off. We accept that on 29 October Mr Brown proposed a compensation payment of £16,500 to Mr Hay, which Mr Hay dismissed. We accept that Mr Hay was angry at that time and intimated that he would work independently from the head coach's room. We are satisfied that he said this in a defiant way, intimating that he intended to be independent of Mr Brown.

The Tribunal also accept that on 30 October, after being advised by Mr Hay that he had not changed his mind on matters, Mr Brown then dismissed the applicant.

The Tribunal then had to apply the law to the facts as they had assessed them. The key element in any employment contract is an implied term of mutual trust and confidence. This is always considered very carefully by any industrial tribunal.

The Tribunal went on to say:

> The actings of Mr Hay had to be considered in the light of this implied term. It is difficult to see how an employee who indicates on more than one occasion that he can no longer work for the company, advises the employer that he will tell him on a particular day whether he will leave or stay, advises him on that day that he wished to leave but wants a pay-off, finds that pay-off unsatisfactory and indicates that because of that he will continue to work independently with his immediate superior can fail to be in breach of the implied term of mutual trust and confidence. It is difficult to see a more blatant breach of the term. The term has been stated in all the cases to be a reciprocal term. The conduct of either an employer or an employee has to be considered objectively. When considered objectively, it is the view of the Tribunal that the actings of Mr Hay must not only have caused serious damage to the relationship between the employer and the employee, but have destroyed it.
>
> Accordingly, the Tribunal were satisfied that the employers were justified in regarding the actings of Mr Hay as being in breach of the implied term of mutual trust and confidence.

Later in the decision it was stated:

> The Tribunal also considered whether the respondents took enough care to satisfy themselves that the applicant was genuine

in his desire to leave and was not just using a threat of leaving as a negotiating ploy. We took into account the relationship between Mr Brown and Mr Hay. They had known each other for a long time.

A discussion on the financial terms had gone on for a period of months. Mr Brown had assessed Mr Hay's attitude and demeanour and was satisfied that Mr Hay was genuinely angry at the terms he had been offered, considering them inadequate. The Tribunal were satisfied that on 27 October, Mr Brown effectively warned Mr Hay about his actions in proposing a pay-off. The Tribunal are satisfied that any reasonable employee, especially an employee of the seniority of Mr Hay, must have known what Mr Brown was saying when Mr Brown said words to the effect that he 'was putting the employment relationship in jeopardy' or 'this was a slippery slope' or 'this was making things impossible'. These were the phrases Mr Brown said he used at that meeting.

It is the Tribunal's opinion that any reasonable employee applying his mind properly must have known what Mr Brown was saying at the meeting on Monday, 27 October. This was that if a satisfactory financial pay-off could not be reached then the employment relationship could not be continued We were absolutely clear that Mr Hay had made up his mind to leave.

Mr Brown had tried to advise him not to leave for pragmatic reasons and warned Mr Hay of the consequences of putting to the board a proposal that he would receive a pay-off if no figure could be agreed. Mr Hay confirmed that he was adamant that he wished to go down that road.

In all the circumstances, therefore, we do not consider the employers erred procedurally in this case.

A substantial extract of the text of the industrial tribunal decision has been presented since not too much of it made headlines when the judgement was issued. It is extremely galling to have to live with adverse and sometimes aggressive references to David Hay for a period of eight months, then to find your position totally vindicated by an independent body at the end of that period, only for the coverage to turn out to be so minimal.

I had been very anxious not to expose David Hay to the full details of the background to his departure from Celtic but I suffered for some considerable time and hoped to have the satisfaction of the public being made aware of my being exonerated completely at the end of the day. But because of the low-key, sketchy coverage, the result scarcely had that effect. I was even subjected to suggestions from those who had not had the benefit of reading the full tribunal judgement that I had used my legal expertise to ensure that David could not win the case, the implication being that the victory was technical and Pyrrhic.

I was particularly uneasy about the problem relating to the removal of scouting records from Celtic Park when David took his belongings away. It took until 17 February 1998 for these records to be returned to Celtic Park. It was done at 10.25 p.m. and David prevailed upon one of the security men who received the goods to sign a receipt saying 'I confirm that I have received all copies of match/player reports as compiled by David Hay whilst employed by Celtic Football Club from July 1994 until October 1997'. How in the world could a security officer know whether he had received all copies of such reports?

There were also suggestions, which came to nothing, about Wim Jansen and Murdo MacLeod giving evidence before the tribunal. By that time both had left the club, and while it made a very good headline, it carried little substance since neither Wim nor Murdo was in any position at all to give any substantive evidence relating to the matter.

All in all, this was a thoroughly sad and unpleasant episode, but I still wish Davie well for the future.

CHAPTER 11

Don't Say 'No' to Lunch

The first home Old Firm match of my time at Celtic Park was scheduled to take place on Wednesday, 19 November, following the original postponement because of the tragic death of the Princess of Wales. Sadly, I did not see the game live. That morning I experienced a tingling down my arm and tremors from my shoulder to my hand. It wasn't the first time I had experienced such sensations but this time they were more pronounced and troubled me enough to justify making a telephone call to the club doctor, Jack Mulhearn, at his surgery around lunchtime. Jack's response was to order me to attend his surgery in the city immediately and he asked if I could get someone to drive me there. I protested that there would be no difficulty whatsoever in driving and, with some difficulty, managed to persuade him.

After conducting some initial tests in his surgery, Jack was concerned enough to want me to attend the Western Infirmary for more detailed examination. The worry was that there might be some heart trouble or the suggestion of a stroke.

I was conscious of causing something of a stir as I walked into the hospital and was concerned that the hospital press office should liaise with Peter McLean at Celtic in connection with any necessary press information. The treatment I then received was absolutely first class, with a number of tests being conducted on me. I was told that either I had suffered a slight stroke or that there was a problem involving discs high up in my spine. Further tests were required to establish the position. I was then taken to the Stroke Unit in the hospital, which obviously must have caused a degree of interest among people within the hospital, both staff and members of the public.

Eventually the tests established that the problem was not a stroke but, indeed, discs in my spine. What was required by way of treatment amounted to physiotherapy and nothing more daunting. Initially the doctors wanted me to stay in the hospital overnight but when the results of the tests were known I persuaded them that I should be allowed to leave. Permission was granted subject to the condition that I did not go to the match at Celtic Park but instead went straight home to rest. By 6.30 p.m. I was home, comforted by the fact that the match was being shown live on television. I did my back no good whatsoever when I leapt off the couch to greet Alan Stubbs heading home a last-minute equaliser.

Meantime, there had been some confusion in the Western Infirmary press office, as a result of which information was provided to the effect that I was still an in-patient in the hospital and had suffered a heart attack. That explains the reports which appeared that evening and the next day, claiming that I was suffering from a major health scare.

After a day at home I was back at work on the Friday and there has been no recurrence of the problem. Everyone was quick to leap on the theory, however, that any health problems were the direct result of the pressure of the job at Celtic. I must confess that despite all the trials and tribulations of working at Celtic, I never felt enough pressure to make me concerned about damage to my health.

Around the turn of the year I was provided with yet another stark example of how some sections of the media operate. The Celtic public relations department received a telephone invitation from a *Daily Mail* journalist called Alan Fraser inviting me and my brother Craig to lunch early in the New Year. When this was presented to me I was immediately somewhat reluctant, because Craig and I had always agreed that we would be extremely cautious about any media activity linking us together. A return call was made to Mr Fraser for further clarification of the purposes of the interview and he apparently indicated that he wanted to do a general feature based on the fact that 1998 was going to be a big year for both of us: Craig was facing the World Cup finals in France, and I was heavily engaged in attempting to help Celtic prevent Rangers from winning their tenth championship in a row. I had a quick word with Craig and we agreed that we should adhere to our original policy of avoiding journalistic pieces linking us in this particular manner, so Mr Fraser received a polite response thanking him for his invitation but declining.

Bearing in mind the host of requests received at that time for one-to-one interviews, not all of which could be accommodated, there was no reason to think about the matter any further. Obviously, the *Daily Mail* in London was not a newspaper I was likely to see, but in the course of a telephone conversation with David Pleat, he asked me what I had done to offend the *Daily Mail*. He told me that a lengthy piece had appeared in that newspaper saying what a wonderful person Craig was and, in summary, what a total swine I was.

Our public relations department obtained a copy of the newspaper with the article in question and, sure enough, the whole thrust of the article was how different Craig and I were in that he was such a charming, friendly fellow whereas I was a pig. Interesting, this, because while I would recognise Alan Fraser, I cannot recollect at any time ever having had a conversation with him. Presumably he felt justified in this slaughter piece because I had declined his invitation to lunch! I suppose he wasn't aware that Craig was totally in agreement with me that the invitation should be declined. In any event, I wrote to the editor of the newspaper in London with a very brief item for his letters page in which I observed that such an outrageously vicious piece seemed to be a very heavy penalty for declining an invitation to lunch with one of his journalists.

The arrival of Harald Brattbakk on 11 December was designed to complete the team jigsaw. The new discipline imposed by Wim Jansen on the defensive unit had started to pay off. The head coach had quickly abandoned the preferred 3–4–3 system with which the team had come to grief in the opening league match against Hibernian. The adjustments made for the second league match, at home to Dunfermline, also failed to provide the correct result and a 2–1 defeat had left Celtic facing the possibility of losing the first three league matches of the season for the first time in history. Happily that had been averted, with a good win, based on a couple of heroic saves from Jonathan Gould at McDiarmid Park against St Johnstone, followed by a Henrik Larsson flying header and a wonderful swerving 20-yarder from Darren Jackson.

The postponement of the first Old Firm match of the season was probably no bad thing at the time. But a key match turned out to be Marc Rieper's debut against Motherwell at Fir Park in mid-September. Motherwell have over the years regularly provided problems for Celtic even when their own form has been poor and a fighting performance by the Fir Park men left them with a 2–1 lead. Jackie McNamara had been out of favour with Wim Jansen and was on the bench for that match. He came on for the second half and completely transformed the game. Craig Burley scored twice and Simon Donnelly won the match with a marvellous twisting header, but this was the match which established Jackie McNamara as a key man wide on the right-hand side of a four-man midfield and set him up to become the Scottish Professional Footballers' Association Player of the Year at the end of the season.

A solid back four of Boyd, Rieper, Stubbs and Mahe became established and Wim would have no truck with any chances being taken in defence. That restricted the attacking instincts of the two full-backs but made for a more dependable rearguard.

The McNamara-inspired comeback at Fir Park came just before the first-leg match against Liverpool in the UEFA Cup. Celtic supporters faced that prospect, I think, with a substantial degree of trepidation. These feelings were enhanced in the opening fifteen minutes when Liverpool totally dominated and Michael Owen scored a superb opportunist goal. Celtic were struggling to have a kick at the ball in that spell.

Suddenly, though, the players began to acquire confidence. They settled and began to compete extremely effectively in all areas of the pitch. By the time Jackie McNamara scored a marvellous equaliser early in the second half, it was no more than we deserved. A Simon Donnelly penalty kick provided a lead which was at that stage richly deserved. It turned out to be a very impressive performance, spoiled only by Steve McManaman's wonder goal in the final minute which, crucially, gave Liverpool two away goals. But I think this was a game which instilled belief in the players that they could compete at the top level, and that had a beneficial effect on league performances.

In the Coca-Cola Cup a slightly fortuitous victory against St John-stone at Perth was the major break in a run which took the club past Berwick Rangers, Motherwell, St Johnstone and then Dunfermline to the final against Dundee United at the end of November.

Injuries and suspensions meant a recast team for the second leg at Anfield against Liverpool. Wim Jansen changed the system very effec-tively to have three central defenders and two wing-backs. An excellent all-round performance almost provided victory, but Simon Donnelly missed a good, if awkward, chance from the edge of the penalty box and we failed to snatch the goal which would have been good enough in the light of an excellent defensive performance.

But credibility had suddenly been restored after that awful league start. Henrik Larsson and Simon Donnelly were playing very effectively up front, although we remained constantly concerned about the lack of cover in the event of injury. That was where Brattbakk came in. He had been watched several times the previous season by David Hay, who hadn't been able to make up his mind whether or not he would be the answer.

There had been lots of chin-stroking and ceiling examination as names were canvassed in the coach's room. A serious attempt was made to acquire the services of a European international striker but his club would not part with him at any price at that particular time. Eventually, David Hay was prevailed upon to travel to Norway to watch Brattbakk play in a Champions' League match for Rosenborg. He came back with a tape of the match which was then examined by Wim Jansen.

It had taken some time to get to that point. David Hay was the man who was always referred to as having a dossier of names of potential recruits for the club. The dossier was very light as far as strikers were concerned. When he mentioned the name Brattbakk again he also indicated that he had personal knowledge of Erik Soler, Harald's agent. Contact was made and a tape was promised. After some delay the tape arrived. It comprised a compilation of goals scored by Harald over four or five seasons. His goalscoring record was truly remarkable, working out at virtually a goal a game over several seasons. His scoring record in the Champions' League was also impressive.

When Davie returned after watching him live, once again he passed the opinion that he thought there had been enough improvement from the previous season to justify his purchase. After Wim Jansen watched the tape, he sanctioned an attempt to try to bring Brattbakk to the club. He did so despite the fact that he had told me at the outset that he distrusted video tapes and always preferred to have first-hand knowledge of a player.

Harald's visit to Glasgow on the first weekend of November proved to be entirely successful in that he was very happy with what he saw of Glasgow and, more importantly, of Celtic Park. Terms were agreed subject to finalising details with Rosenborg and the completion of the league section of the European Champions' Cup. Two visits to Trondheim in Norway were required in order to reach an agreement but everything was cleared for Harald to travel to Glasgow on 11 December to sign – subject to one factor.

The club has a policy whereby a player costing a seven-figure fee should be watched live at least six times by more than one representative of the club. Since one of those required to watch a player in these circumstances had to be the head coach all that was necessary was for Wim Jansen to travel to watch Brattbakk play and approve the deal.

I reminded Wim of the policy and suggested that I could make arrangements for him to watch Brattbakk play in a Champions' League match, but Wim indicated that he had been invited as a guest to watch Feyenoord play Manchester United at Old Trafford and could not watch Brattbakk at the same time. There was a further opportunity to watch Harald play two weeks later and I raised the matter with Wim again at the appropriate time. On this occasion he indicated that he was not prepared to miss any training sessions to travel to Trondheim for the match.

I raised this with Fergus McCann because I respected Wim's dedication to attending all training sessions. It was agreed that we would arrange for a private jet to take Wim to Norway immediately after training on Wednesday morning, returning him to Glasgow after the match on Wednesday night so that he could be at training on Thursday morning. There were two possible flights. One was a very lengthy flight, whereas the other, with a more powerful aeroplane and costing more than double the price, could get him there and back much more quickly. Fergus agreed that the more expensive option should be taken.

When I put that proposition to Wim, he stately simply that he was not going. When I reminded him about the club policy, he said, 'But it's not my policy.' He was adamant that his examination of the video tape and David Hay's live sighting was enough for him to authorise the purchase, but I knew exactly the kind of reception I could expect when I explained this to the directors – an unfavourable one. I was right.

My recommendation to the board was that the transaction should still proceed and after substantial discussion it was agreed on the understanding that the policy could not be breached again at a later time. I was instructed to explain this to the head coach. It was on that basis that the transfer of Harald Brattbakk to Celtic was completed on 11 December and I hoped and prayed that the prolific goalscorer the club was seeking had been acquired.

Wim kept Harald on the bench for the first four matches after his arrival, bringing him on for short periods towards the end. Eventually, he started the Scottish Cup tie against Morton in January and broke his scoring duck. Four against Kilmarnock in a league match shortly afterwards suggested that we had a new hero wearing number nine in our midst. That performance was followed by another two fine goals against Dunfermline – and that was a signal for David Hay to contribute once again to the *Sunday Mail* by talking about Harald Brattbakk being his legacy to Celtic.

I can think of no finer gentleman in the game of football than Harald Brattbakk. He is intelligent, committed and dedicated but, like many others before him and many others to come, he had substantial difficulty in coming to terms with the size and scale of Celtic. The vital importance of every match, the goldfish-bowl effect in Glasgow and the constant vacillation between triumph and tragedy all take a bit of getting used to. So does the media interest.

When Harald attended a club-inspired event to support ethnic minorities, he found himself facing a number of journalists who, the following day, claimed that he believed that finishing second in the league would be acceptable. He was totally aghast. He had been the victim of a huddle. Such was his standing among the rest of the players that they were furious. A man who could not do enough to support the charitable aims of Celtic was so disenchanted that he indicated he felt compelled to withdraw from any further press dealings. I sympathised.

By that time, in April, goals had become hard to come by as the team began to stutter towards the climax of the season. But whatever happens in Harald's career, he will never be forgotten as the man who scored the vital second goal in the final league match of the season at Celtic Park against St Johnstone. The acceleration and finish suggested very high hopes for the season ahead, but once again poor Harald found it extremely difficult to accept the many opportunities he received at the start of the new season to establish himself as the goal machine the vast Celtic support was dying to acclaim.

Wim Jansen's failure to implement club policy in going to see Harald Brattbakk live was another indication of the difficulties the club was experiencing as far as the head coach's position was concerned. He was taciturn, largely uncommunicative and clearly a victim of the constant badgering he appeared to be receiving about the modesty of Celtic's ambitions, their penny-pinching approach and their unwillingness to go into the market for big-time players.

No one had more of his ear than Murdo MacLeod. Murdo appeared never to get his mind round the new structure which had been put in place at the club. He had locked into Wim Jansen immediately. My perception was that he had decided that his fortunes would be best served by getting as close as possible to the head coach. He did that all right. By mid-October he had clearly established himself as Wim's right-hand man. He sought a meeting with me and told me that he thought he should receive a better salary. He told me that he had one of the top four jobs in Scottish football and was not being paid accordingly. He claimed that Archie Knox, whom he considered to be his equivalent at Rangers, was much more highly paid.

I explained to him that assessing his job as one of the top four in Scotland failed to take into account the new structure which had been put in place. Walter Smith at Rangers was still functioning as an old-style British football manager and Archie Knox was his deputy. At Celtic, Wim Jansen had no responsibility whatsoever for any type of management outside coaching the first team and preparing the team for matches. Murdo was his deputy in that respect. The point appeared to be lost on him.

It was then that he made the statement which has haunted me ever since. In support of his request for more money he said, 'I could be a hundred per cent more supportive of you if I had a better deal.' I stopped in my tracks. I could not believe that I had heard correctly. I asked him if he would repeat what he had just said. He did so in precisely the same terms.

The import of what he had said did not appear to occur to him. I told him that the implication was that he was not giving one hundred per cent now and needed more money to do so. In these circumstances he was effectively cheating in not giving his best. I further explained that my understanding of the position was that when you took up a new post you worked as hard as you possibly could to render yourself indispensable, achieve some success and then look for some reward. It was not appropriate to imply that you would do the job at half-cock for the money on offer and would only step up a gear and give your all when the remuneration package was improved.

I had known Murdo for many years. This, for me, was a new side to his character. I was flabbergasted. Under no circumstances was I prepared to accede to that kind of approach and I told him it was much too early to consider a salary review, although I was prepared to look at his bonus position.

Our relationship never recovered from that exchange. I never looked upon him the same way afterwards. In most employment situations anyone saying what he said could have expected dismissal immediately. I was tempted, but realised that it was not a viable option, bearing in mind the difficulties being experienced with David Hay and the closeness to Wim Jansen of both David and Murdo. The normal rules of industry and employment do not apply blindly within an organisation like Celtic where even more goes under the microscope.

If you were cynical, you could wonder if there had been a concerted attempt by both Murdo and Davie to use the connection they had established with Wim Jansen in order to ensure that a request for more money could not be rejected.

I have often wondered what would have happened had I managed to obtain more money for Murdo at that time. Would he have been one hundred per cent more supportive? What effect might that have had on the overall situation at the club? Would he have had a positive influence on Wim Jansen as far as the club was concerned? Would he have offered an olive branch to the development coaching staff? Would he then have supported the club's initiative under the banner 'Aware and Confident', whereby a detailed document was prepared and a seminar arranged as a guide for coaching staff on the difficulties of dealing with young players in the modern age? Would he have been a more positive influence with the players in respect of their attitude to club-initiated events? Would he have eliminated the constant ticket difficulties occasioned by his distribution of complimentaries in such a way that MacLeod guests were regularly prominent? One hundred per cent more supportive means he is starting from scratch, and the clear impression I derived was that scratch was exactly where we were.

Results were beginning to go well and I was certainly not prepared to allow anything to interfere with that. But I knew that trouble was being stored up and the day of reckoning would arrive.

CHAPTER 12

Time for Appeasement

Wim Jansen was appointed as Celtic's first ever head coach. His responsibilities were principally confined to the first team and on-field performances. However, in order to carry out that function properly, it appeared to me essential for the head coach to relate readily to all the coaches on the staff and to acquaint himself with the young players at the club who were aspiring to force their way into the first-team squad.

This was not an area which appeared to generate much interest from Wim. I can safely say that this was a major disappointment to the development coaches within the club, who had looked forward to having the opportunity to learn from someone they hoped would prove to be a Dutch master. One of the common features of all the coaches I have met is that they are generally massively interested in what other coaches are doing and what techniques are being developed at home and abroad. That is certainly the case for the development coaches at Celtic.

To see them shunned so blatantly by Wim and Murdo MacLeod was a matter of great sadness to me but much more so to them. Quite apart from the obvious disappointment of apparently not being worthy of routine communication from the top man, they found themselves working in something of a vacuum, constantly feeling intensive tacit disapproval from the head coach without any substance being communicated.

Disappointment felt by excellent men like Eric Black, Willie McStay, Kenny McDowall and Tom O'Neill was obvious. They found themselves in substantial difficulty when people outside the club asked them what they had learned from Wim Jansen. Loyalty frequently led them to give fudged responses as though attempting to retain the privacy of the information gleaned but the reality was that they had felt totally unwelcome following earlier approaches to try to learn something of the Dutchman's techniques.

Only the tight cabal of those involved with the first team appeared to be given the time of day by Wim. These included Brian Scott, conditioning instructor Jim Hendry, masseur Graham Quinn, Danny McGrain and Peter Latchford and, of course, David Hay and Murdo. Add to that select group on appropriate occasions Dr Jack Mulhearn and the set was complete. Even the backroom staff's Christmas night out in 1997 excluded the rest of the coaching staff, who did not receive an invitation. When the development staff had their night out, invitations to Wim's set were declined, with the creditable exceptions of Danny McGrain and Peter Latchford.

Shortly before Christmas that year the directors had a meeting with those heading the technical side of the club in order to obtain a briefing and learn about plans for development of the footballing side of the operation. It was agreed, in particular, that Eric Black would present details of his proposals to strengthen the development side of the club with the purpose of trying to bring through more homegrown players.

Eric prepared a presentation document outlining his plans and distributed these among all those attending the meeting before addressing everyone by taking them through his development proposals and answering questions. The presentation was impressive, including such details as the appointment of a new education officer, the former player John Cushley, and a host of other initiatives which he had created with the help of Willie McStay and the rest of the development team.

There was a lively discussion around the table about the issues raised by Eric's paper and eventually Wim Jansen was asked for his observations. 'I must have about fifteen of these documents at home,' he said. 'The only important thing is the quality of the coaching.'

The tone of the whole meeting was instantly changed. People clearly felt uncomfortable. Eric Black was thoroughly embarrassed. There was a lot of shuffling in chairs. My interpretation was that everyone realised how dismissive and unkind the comment was. There was also nothing constructive about the observation and in fact no comment was ever obtained about the paper itself from the head coach. Wim did himself no favours with that reaction to what amounted to a very substantial amount of work on the part of Eric Black.

Interestingly, the following day Eric approached Wim and said that he was extremely interested to note that he had fifteen such documents in his possession and wondered if he would be kind enough to let him have a look at them in order to see what he could learn. At that point

Wim had to confess that he didn't actually have any such documents, although he had seen a number of them in the past.

By this time it had become clearly established that there was to be no cross-fertilisation of any kind between the first-team squad and the other players at the club. Training schedules had to be set up so that reserves and youths did not interfere with first-team activities and no youth players were integrated into the first-team set-up as a reward for good performances or to provide experience.

So when the opportunity arose for the club to consider bringing in some teenagers from Argentina, there was no initial requirement to consult the head coach as he had made it clear that he had no interest in anything outside first-team matters. Eric Black went on a fact-finding mission to Argentina for a week and watched a host of young players, as a result of which half a dozen were invited to Glasgow to join the youths' training to establish if any of them could be integrated into the Celtic development system.

Wim Jansen was not consulted. He probably should have been, and certainly would have been, had circumstances been different. However, he had made it so clear that he wanted nothing whatsoever to do with the coaches involved with the reserves and youths that there appeared to be no need to involve him in consideration of teenage players who were certainly not instant first-team material.

The head coach said nothing and asked no questions. Only at a later time did he complain bitterly about not being told about the Argentinians, but he made it clear that he had no wish to be involved by a display of huffiness which was quite remarkable.

Constantly at his elbow, encouraging him with every move he made and doing nothing to improve the situation was the ubiquitous Mr MacLeod.

It was clear that the kind of unity which I was targeting was unlikely to be achievable within the prevailing regime. This was a major disappointment. My vision for the future of Celtic technically was a hierarchy of coaches with Wim Jansen at the top and people below him who would be capable, in due course, of succeeding him, very much in the mould of Liverpool. My hope was that Wim would see out his three-year contract, perhaps extend it, but in due course be succeeded by someone already on the club's coaching staff. My initial thought way back in June/July 1997 was that the likely candidate was Murdo MacLeod. Further down the line, bearing in mind the approval obtained from Wim and Murdo to bring in Eric Black to lead development, it could be possible that Eric or Willie McStay could be Celtic head coaches at some point in the years ahead. That dream was crumbling on the surly and largely uncommunicative Wim Jansen, aided by the man whose industry and integrity, in my opinion, did not appear to match his ambition, Murdo MacLeod.

By this time, around December 1997, I was convinced that Wim Jansen had no intention of staying longer than one season at Celtic. That had been his initial wish and every move he was making was consistent with not seeking to extend his stay beyond the end of the season. Why, otherwise, would he have shown such trifling interest in young players at the club? Why was he not communicating urgently his needs to eager young coaches at his disposal? And why was he showing such reluctance towards communication with members of staff and club officials? In addition, Murdo had not received the better deal which would have made him one hundred per cent more supportive and it was certainly apparent that he had failed to take any positive message from our meeting in October.

The situation, in management terms, was massively difficult, again bearing in mind the glare of publicity and the absolute necessity of halting Rangers' bid for ten in a row. I took the decision to embark upon a policy of appeasement until the end of the season. In the interests of winning the championship, which was becoming an increasingly likely possibility, I was convinced that it was my duty to do everything possible to avoid ruffling feathers and simply keep the head coach happy at virtually all costs until the final match was over. There was a growing impression in my mind that Wim would not be too troubled about the team's failure as long as no blame for such failure was attributed to him.

Accordingly, it was imperative for me to provide him with my total support, without insisting upon club policy being implemented or trying to resolve any internal difficulties in a manner which might have caused any strife. It was a decision which I believed was absolutely correct given the very unusual circumstances, but it virtually killed me to pursue it.

I also struggled to cope with the head coach's response to a polite enquiry after a struggling 1–1 draw against Motherwell at Fir Park in January. That was a match in which Paul Lambert scored a spectacular long-range effort to earn a draw, this coming not long after his equally spectacular second goal against Rangers to win the Old Firm derby at New Year.

After the match at Motherwell I asked Wim for his theory on why we found it so difficult to cope with a fighting team like Motherwell when they didn't have the type of quality player wearing Celtic colours. 'It is simply a lack of quality,' he said. 'When matches like that are very tight we simply don't have the necessary quality to make the difference.'

I was amazed at my success in curbing my incredulity. What I was unable to refrain from asking him was the name of any player in the Motherwell team who he thought might improve our team on the basis that I would then attempt to buy him. 'Oh, no, there are none,' he said.

However, our decent run was continuing and the championship had become a real possibility. It was even more important that the policy of appeasement continued and nothing was allowed to rock the boat.

The media had backed off somewhat and I was able to enjoy what was obviously only the lull before the storm. I can only recall one idiotic story appearing in a Sunday newspaper suggesting that I had to be prevailed upon not to come off the team bus after the Coca-Cola Cup final carrying the trophy. I wondered where that load of nonsense came from. I do not even recall touching the trophy on the bus and I adhered to my normal policy throughout the season of leaving the team bus after all the players and coaches.

The lull ended at a point shortly afterwards when *The Herald* carried a story claiming that Wim and I were at odds and did not get on well. The story declared that Wim resented my 'interference' on football matters. There were no quotes from anyone and no source was identified.

Clearly, the correct thing to do in the interests of the club was to defuse that story by issuing appropriate statements, principally from Wim but also from me. But Wim did not want to say anything. He argued that he only ever gave press conferences pre- and post-match and could see no basis for departing from that policy now. I saw the logic in that and offered no objection, although there were other pressures from within the club imposed upon Wim, using the argument that it would be the first question asked at the pre-match press conference the coming Friday. He still would not budge.

I issued a statement indicating that when I had been involved in the process of identifying a suitable head coach for Celtic, I was not looking for someone who would be my best pal or someone who would be my companion for a pint after work in the evening. That was, indeed, the case. One of the things which always fascinated Fergus McCann, in particular, was the fact that so many posts at football clubs were filled by someone's pal. If you think about it, he is right.

When a manager is appointed, he seldom wants to keep the previous backroom staff, instead wanting to appoint his own pals and associates into positions where he knows he can trust them and they will not be trying to knife him in the back. It is not the way things work in industry or in commerce but it certainly appears to be the case in football.

Under no circumstances would that have been allowed to be the case at Celtic, and rightly so. The idea was to try to identify the best possible man for the job and to try to ensure that there was a working relationship, even if there was no social relationship. In my entire time at Celtic I never once dined at the home of any club official or employee, nor did they with me. But that did not stop good working relationships and many strong friendships being created.

Sure enough, at the first press conference attended by Wim later that week, the issue of our relationship was raised. I pushed the line about not looking for someone to have a pint with and Wim said as little as possible. However, he was pressed quite forcibly on the question of alleged interference on my part with his football responsibilities.

'Has there been any interference at all in footballing matters from Jock Brown?' he was asked.

'No,' he responded, quietly.

He certainly did not elaborate but he could not have been more unequivocal.

After Wim had left the conference, I asked the journalists why they sought to insult him by trying to suggest that he would allow someone like me to interfere with his conduct of team matters. 'Do you really believe he is the type of man who would allow someone like me to influence how he runs the team?' I clearly remember saying. 'He would simply walk out if that kind of interference existed.'

There was no comeback from those attending the conference. Yet several of those present on that occasion have continued to refer to my interference with team matters, ignoring Wim Jansen's unequivocal denial. It really was a matter of immense frustration to me but I don't remember his negative response to interference being reported in many publications. It would appear to suit the purpose better to have that theory still fluttering around to generate comment, discussion and controversy.

While things had become more difficult between us, and the relationship was, to say the least, uneasy, Wim was not interested in communicating and I had substantial difficulty with appeasement. However, there were pressing matters which required our joint attention, such as the recruitment of new players to improve the first-team squad for the season ahead. The time had come to take advantage of the Bosman ruling and consider the possibility of out-of-contract players joining us in the summer. I was most anxious to become involved in pre-contracts with suitable players and needed the head coach's co-operation to identify potential targets.

Accordingly, I arranged a meeting with Wim on the morning of 12 March 1998 when the only item on the agenda was personnel for the following season. Wim had already made it perfectly clear after the signing of Harald Brattbakk that he was content with his squad for that particular championship campaign and had no thoughts about bringing in new players. He had even told the press earlier in March that he would not be seeking to bring in new players before the transfer deadline at the end of the month.

At our meeting I told him that I was anxious to have a good holiday this summer, and that meant identifying new players required for next season and tying up contracts as soon as possible. In order to do so I needed to make a detailed report to the board of directors relating to Wim's assessment of the playing squad and identification of potential new recruits. I told him that I needed from him a detailed appraisal of the current playing squad with particular regard to those who might be surplus to requirements, along with identification of the areas of the team requiring improvement and, ideally, names of players he fancied.

Wim listened to me as I outlined in detail what was required so that I could obtain the necessary budget from the board for his recruitment plans. I realised it was largely a monologue, because he offered little contribution until I had finished. 'I am not interested,' he said. 'I don't work that way.'

Remembering my policy of appeasement, I suggested gently to him that we would have to work that way in order to obtain budget approval from the board. 'All I want to know is how much money I will have to spend,' he said.

'It's not that simple,' I replied. 'The board will not sanction a substantial sum of money for spending on players without receiving from you the information which I have outlined. I do believe, though, that if we present a good, detailed report I will be able to obtain for us their complete backing.'

'I am still not interested,' he said.

I explained to him that in the event of him not being prepared to co-operate by providing the necessary detailed information, the chances were that we would not be able to obtain any budget at all for strengthening the team. His response was the equivalent of a shrug of the shoulders.

I knew at that moment that there was no possibility of him staying at the club. Nevertheless, I asked him to consider the matter carefully and told him the date of the next board meeting at which our recruitment plans would be discussed if a report could be submitted. It was clear that I was wasting my time.

CHAPTER 13

The 'Get~Out' Clause

Nine days later Craig Burley's first penalty kick for the club earned us three vital points against Aberdeen at Pittodrie, making up for the disappointment six days earlier when we dropped two points at home in a televised game against Dundee United. Craig volunteered for the kick because Simon Donnelly wasn't playing and the club's other regular penalty-taker, Andreas Thom, had departed for Hertha Berlin at the end of January. The pressure in relation to the championship challenge was mounting.

That day in Aberdeen I was alerted to the fact that there was a story appearing in the press the following day about a 'get-out clause' in Wim Jansen's contract, saying that he might not stay at the club after the season's end. Sure enough, such a story was splashed all over the back page of the *Sunday Mail* the following day. It talked about both Wim Jansen and Murdo MacLeod. It indicated that Wim Jansen had a get-out clause at the end of the season and may well exercise this and leave the club. It also indicated that Murdo MacLeod was unhappy with his lot, in particular because he did not have a contract. The plot thickened.

Mindful of Wim's position when it came to departing from his usual policy of pre- and post-match press conferences, I had to deal with that particular story on the Sunday myself. I issued a statement in which I said that the details of Wim Jansen's contract were confidential but that he had expressed no dissatisfaction to me at any time. Further, I indicated that I could not understand the reference to Murdo MacLeod because he had signed two contracts since arriving at Celtic, one as reserve team coach and another as assistant head coach when he had been given that appointment by Wim. That obviously struck a nerve. I have no doubt that Murdo was asked for his reaction to my comments about him signing two contracts and that was a fact he simply could not deny. Our relationship deteriorated further.

I was extremely concerned about the disruptive effect of allowing such inflammatory material to reach the public domain at a time when the club had a very real chance of winning the championship.

At that point Wim astonished me. On the Monday evening it was brought to my attention that he had given an interview on the club hotline in which he confirmed the get-out clause and expressed his concern about the fact that the club had not approached him with a view to taking the contract into the following season. I was told that he had given the interview on the clear understanding that it would not be edited in any way. It was then presented to me on the Monday evening on the basis that it could either be stopped by the club or used in its entirety.

I considered the matter very carefully indeed. All my instincts are against censorship and I was once a card-carrying member of the National Union of Journalists. At the same time, I knew that if the material were used on the hotline it would be all over the following day's papers. Similarly, if the club blocked the material, it appeared to me inevitable that Wim would still issue the same information at the pre-match press conference the following Friday since he had obviously made it perfectly clear that he wanted this information in the public domain. I decided to let the tape run on the basis that we would attempt to deal with the consequences of the press coverage the following day.

The whole affair was, indeed, sinister. Wim's contract provided that from 1 April 1998 discussions would take place with a view to both parties agreeing to kick in the remainder of his contract, or otherwise. There was accordingly no justification whatsoever for any discussions to have been contemplated by the time he allowed this information to reach the public domain. There had to be other reasons behind the sudden departure from the policy of giving only pre- and post-match conferences to which he had adhered rigidly since his arrival.

What was abundantly clear was that this was not in the club's interests. However, it did set up a perfect excuse if the championship challenge failed. Similarly, if the championship challenge succeeded, it would have succeeded despite the apparently trying circumstances under which Wim and Murdo operated.

I understood clearly the implications there and then. Wim could not lose. I could not win. Either he won the championship and became a hero, or he lost the championship and it was all my fault. It was put to me in precisely these terms by one of the international players in the team.

My choice was simple. I could try to look after my own position by attacking Wim and Murdo there and then while the championship race was uncertain, or I could continue my policy of appeasement in the overall interests of winning the championship. There was really no choice to make. The championship had to be won.

It had become clear to me, however, that my policy of appeasement had to go even further. It was important that I communicated with Wim as little as possible in order to avoid any kind of disruption or confrontation. I did have to communicate with him, however, on one particular player issue. That related to Malky Mackay. A more decent, hardworking, committed professional it would be hard to find. His frustration was mounting because he had been excluded from all squads since September 1997 and it was clear to him that he was no longer featuring in Wim's plans.

I knew that to be the case and following discussions with Malky I asked the head coach if he would sanction a loan for the big centre-half for the remainder of the season. 'Make sure he only goes to a good club,' Wim said, to his great credit.

I then became involved in substantial negotiations lasting the best part of a week, as a result of which it was agreed that he would go on loan to Huddersfield Town for the rest of the season. All the details were sorted out in the middle of a Tuesday afternoon and I realised that it was appropriate to advise Wim of the progress made.

It was between 3.30 and 4.00 p.m. He did not answer his phone at home so I called him on his mobile telephone. He was shopping in the supermarket with his wife, he told me. I advised him that I had now concluded an agreement to allow Malky to go to Huddersfield Town, and Wim went berserk. 'No, no, no!' he shouted on the telephone. 'I don't want him to go.'

I explained to him that we had discussed this several days earlier and he had sanctioned the fact that he could go, as long as he was going to a decent club. Huddersfield Town qualified. He argued in a very agitated fashion that he did not want anyone to leave the club at this stage in the run-in to the championship and he certainly did not want Malky to go. 'If you are selling him, that's different,' he said.

I couldn't really understand the difference from his perspective but I eventually said to him that I needed him to tell me whether or not he would sanction Malky's departure. 'I don't want him to go, but you do what you like,' he bellowed.

The implications of this discussion were obvious. The policy of appeasement was once again under strain. I took the decision to block the move.

I telephoned Malky at home as he was packing his bag. He thought I was calling simply to wish him good luck but I then told him that the head coach would not sanction the move and in these circumstances I could not let it happen. The big fellow was shattered. My heart went out to him. 'I was there when it was agreed that you could negotiate a loan for me,' he said.

'I know,' I said. 'But it appears as though the coach has changed his mind, and I must respect that.'

Malky duly appeared for training the following morning and asked for a meeting with me and Wim. He was clearly very upset and angry but he conducted himself superbly. Wim tried to explain to him that he did not want anyone to leave the club pending the championship run-in, and while he could not answer Malky's observation that he had not seen fit to use him since September the previous year and had sanctioned the move a week earlier, the head coach would not budge. Mind you, he offered no objection to the sale of another fine young man in the squad, Stuart Gray, to Reading just before the transfer deadline date.

It was the second time a proposed loan deal created difficulties between Wim and me. Tommy Johnson had been unfit for most of the season and by the time he had recovered Wim had authorised me to find a club for him in England. Eventually I agreed terms with Steve Coppell at Crystal Palace for Tommy to go on loan there. That discussion was also completed on a Tuesday afternoon. Wim had gone home. I did not telephone him to advise him of the position. I decided I would simply tell him when he arrived for work the following morning.

Unfortunately, Wim bumped into Tommy Johnson before I reached him on the Wednesday morning and Tommy indicated that he was in to collect his boots before heading off to London for discussions with Palace about going there on loan. Wim challenged me about not keeping him fully advised. He was right. It was on that basis that I made certain I made the call to him in the supermarket over the Malky Mackay issue. On that occasion he was wrong.

In any event, the public portrayal of the get-out clause in Wim's contract was that there had been a screw-up on the part of the club in allowing it to be in the contract in the first place, and implementing it in terms of the contract. That was certainly not the case.

In the first instance, Wim had made it clear from the outset that he wanted a one-year contract. We had in turn made it perfectly clear to him that this was not satisfactory from our point of view since we required continuity. It was on that basis that a compromise was reached regarding the wording of the contract, whereby the term was three years and provision was made for a break clause after the first year. The clause worked both ways and my attitude to this was entirely positive. I took the view that if Wim Jansen were a huge success there would be no way in the world he would want to leave a club like Celtic, with its massive support and magnificent facilities. However, if he didn't do well, the get-out clause operated very effectively for the club.

My earnest hope was that towards the end of the first season we would have a five-minute meeting with Wim whereby he would confirm that he was happy to continue as head coach and we would similarly confirm that we were happy to retain him in that capacity, as a result of which the balance of the contract would kick in. No negotiations would be required, since the provisions to operate from the start of year two were already fixed in the contract. All that was required were two nods of the head at the appropriate time.

Obviously, it would have been perfectly in order during these discussions in April for Wim to say that there were certain things he wasn't happy about and an attempt would have been made to resolve them. Generally, the club was entitled to say there were aspects of his work which caused concern, and an attempt could have been made to resolve these too. But for Wim to be quoted on 23 March as saying that he was disappointed that no one from the club had made any approaches to him was entirely inappropriate, bearing in mind the terms of the contract.

However, his outburst on the club hotline on that Monday evening created a sea change in his method of dealing with the media. As I expected, the circus began immediately the hotline was broadcast. The following morning the newspapers presented their version of events. Wim was collared as he returned from training that Tuesday morning and actually made comments to various newspapers. This was something he had never done before. Suddenly, he had gone out of control.

The club was on the back foot, having to make appropriate statements to attempt to defuse the situation. It was not going to be defused. My own view is that Wim was somewhat taken aback by the reaction to his departure from policy because he appeared to become even more uncomfortable about the whole media issue. I was certainly not a happy man. I asked him a number of questions pertaining to what I saw as a blatant breach of contract but I received no answers, not even unsatisfactory ones.

At the Friday pre-match press conference, before a crucial match against Hearts, he made it clear that he would not discuss the matter any further until the championship race was over. He gave no indication at all as to whether he wanted to stay or go. It certainly appeared to be an attempt to defuse the situation in view of the important matches ahead but it was an attempt which clearly failed. I made it clear that I would not comment on the issue at all, pending clarification of Wim's position and the completion of the championship race. Once again, this was a position which I believed to be in the interests of the club, but it was one which was certain to do me no good in the eyes of the media, and thus the supporters.

At that point in the season there were seven league matches remaining, and a cup semi-final was looming against Rangers. I do not believe it is any coincidence that of those remaining eight competitive matches, only three were won. Oh, I know that the players said that they were unaffected by what was going on, but while that may have been true in a conscious sense, I fear that, subconsciously, they were adversely affected by the media circus which didn't end until the last match on 9 May.

There was no occasion when Wim faced the press when he was not asked about his plans for the future. On each occasion he indicated that he would not give his decision until the end of the season. Eventually he started to admit that he had made his decision but that he wasn't telling anyone except his wife.

It would be entirely deceitful for me to say that I was not infuriated by this. He was not prepared to talk to any club officials about his intentions and as far as I was concerned he was treating Celtic with contempt. My view was that it was arrogant and contemptuous for any individual to indicate at a club like Celtic that he would make up his mind whether he was staying or going in his own good time without any dialogue with anyone. The situation was exacerbated by the fact that I believed he was not honouring his obligations or carrying out his duties in full. By that I mean that he had shown total disregard for the club's position regarding the need to strengthen the squad for the new season. I was later castigated for the fact that new players were not being brought in and so was Wim's successor, Jozef Venglos, in circumstances where the blame lay squarely with the head coach who had failed to carry out an essential part of his job for the last three months of his tenure. Even if Wim had known at that time that he was going, which I believe was the case, he still had an obligation to carry out his duties properly until the end of his contract, and that meant restructuring the squad for the new season.

Under some pressure early in April, Wim did indicate that there was little point in him considering what players to bring to the club if he was not going to be there by the time they arrived. That was entirely wrong. He should have given the necessary information about the playing staff and he should have indicated clearly whether his intention was to stay or go. If he had indicated to the club that he intended to go and at the same time had given the information requested about the playing staff, it would have been up to the board of directors to decide whether to follow his recommendations in the knowledge that he would not be there the following season or whether to hold off. Either way, it would have been possible to convey to the supporters what the current state of play was and thus enhance an overall understanding of the situation.

One thing was clear to me throughout this period. In the interests of Celtic winning the championship I could not usefully say anything, despite the fact that I knew this was burying me even deeper in the media hole. However, I was completely convinced that there was no possibility of Wim being at Celtic for the following season. This, as far as I was concerned, meant that urgent action on the head coach front was required. I would have gone ahead discreetly then to set up a new head coach to take over as soon as Wim's inevitable announcement was made, but obviously there were risks attached to that strategy and I was persuaded that all that could be done until an announcement was made by Wim was research into potential candidates. That exercise began immediately.

Around this time we also had to contend with another *Sunday Mail* special. The story they offered this time was the fact that some of our players had wanted to bring in the services of a psychotherapist to help with mental preparation for the run-in but I had intervened and objected. The article mentioned the name of a psychotherapist which meant absolutely nothing to me. At no time had any player either on his own part or on behalf of the rest of the squad approached me about enlisting the aid of such a person.

Once again, the message being conveyed was that there was discord within the Celtic camp and I was supposed to be at the heart of it. In my column in the *Celtic View* I gave the lie to the story and made the point that I had never heard of the psychotherapist who had been quoted. Similarly, no player was able to be quoted to provide any kind of authority to the story. Usually, in such circumstances, credit is given to 'a Celtic insider'. I have always found that term amusing. I am convinced that it frequently means either 'this is something I have just made up', or 'this is information given to me by some disenchanted employee who has his own agenda to pursue'.

In any event, the following Sunday the *Sunday Mail* triumphantly showed a photocopy of a letter to a psychotherapist in England apparently signed by me eight months earlier in which I acknowledged receipt of his original letter offering his services and advised him that the matter would be referred to the head coach for his consideration. According to the *Sunday Mail*, this proved that their story was correct and provided the evidence which, as a lawyer, I always sought to support allegations.

There was no doubt that it was my signature on the letter. However, I still stand by every word I uttered in the *Celtic View*. The volume of mail addressed to me at Celtic Park was substantial. It was so substantial that it required an enormous amount of time to deal with it. On this basis, a number of standard replies were used by my secretary, who typed these and presented them to me for my signature at the end of the day. The standard reply to anyone offering services of the kind involved in this matter was the courteous response which this particular gentleman received. The letter would then be referred to the head coach or, if medical matters were involved, Brian Scott, the physiotherapist.

How my polite letter in August 1997 in response to the psychotherapist's offer of services justified the *Sunday Mail* in April 1998 publishing a story that I was at odds with the players over the use of such services in the run-in to the championship I shall never know. What the psychotherapist was doing providing the *Sunday Mail* with a copy of a letter from me is another question which is unlikely to produce an answer flattering to the man concerned.

This kind of journalism is similar to material emerging from the tabloid journalists' huddle. Nonsense is frequently reported. Then it is repeated by feature writers and columnists who operate on the basis that the information is correct. This involves repeats of the original misinformation. It also becomes the topic of discussion with a countless number of phone-ins and pundits pontificating on radio and television. I have listened to debates about issues which were total fiction which had appeared in tabloid newspapers, and the more often they were repeated and discussed the more credibility they seemed to obtain.

I remember chatting to Gordon Smith at a time when he had a column in the *Daily Express*. It was just after the Di Canio business and

Gordon had written a piece in the *Express* which was absolutely excellent except for one thing — it was based on newspaper reports which were erroneous. When I made that point to Gordon he responded, quite reasonably, to the effect that he really had little option but to write his column based on 'news' which was reported. He had not attended the appropriate press conferences in relation to Di Canio but had simply read reports arising from the 'huddle'. I genuinely sympathise with writers in his position.

The other matter which always caused great concern was the manner in which broadcasting crews, especially television crews, handled issues in the vicinity of the stadium. Television crews have been witnessed outside Celtic Park mustering a crowd of supporters and coaching them on how to display banners and shout slogans against people like Fergus McCann and me. There are always at least a couple of dozen people hanging around the entrance to the stadium, and at the time in the summer when the popular line was that McCann and Brown must go, that entire group would be pulled tightly together by the camera crew, who would then shoot them making their point as though there were hundreds, even thousands, protesting. I suppose it's all about going back to base with a story, any story, which fits the original purpose.

However, during that period in April, the possibility of fixing up Mr Z to take over during the close season emerged. Mr Z was the man I had met in Larnaca on my first day with Celtic. He is a top-class, internationally renowned coach who had been carefully researched the previous summer but who had not been able to obtain release from his contract at that time. I was now contacted by representatives on his behalf, since they were aware of the circus surrounding Wim Jansen, and it was made clear to me that a decision could be taken during the month of April to bring him to the club for the following season. However, if a commitment could not be made to Mr Z during that period then his own contractual situation would almost certainly eliminate the possibility of him being available.

The decision, taken above my head, was that we could not make any commitment to any alternative head coach until Wim Jansen had made his announcement. My own view was that it was abundantly clear what the announcement would be and it was therefore prudent for us to set up his successor to ensure the smoothest of transitions and the longest possible lead-in time for the new coach in advance of the new season. But clearly there were substantial risks to that strategy and it would be entirely wrong for me to say that I went into the trenches fighting my corner when the club view expressed to me was that this was a risk we could not take while the championship race was on. In fact, I was persuaded that this was indeed the correct course of action. I conveyed the news of that decision to Mr Z's representatives and, sure enough, his ensuing contractual position took him out of the running.

CHAPTER 14

The Title, and Jansen Departs

Seven league matches to go and the championship was well within our grasp. It was a situation you would have killed for back in August, especially after the opening two league defeats. The media circus of 23 and 24 March immediately preceded four tough matches: Hearts at home, two matches against Rangers, one in the league and one in the cup, and an away midweek match at Kilmarnock. The last thing the club needed during that period was any distraction.

It was always felt within the club that just before a crunch match, especially against Rangers, some story would appear in the press to destabilise the camp. It got to the stage where I used to joke about this so that it did not come as any surprise when the disruptive story broke. That strategy worked, because it was always a source of some amusement within Celtic Park when the negative story appeared right on cue.

This time, though, we had shot ourselves in the foot. More accurately, Wim Jansen, and those advising him, had shot the club in the foot. I should make it clear that I do not believe for one second that decisions taken about the leaking of the get-out clause, broadcasting on the hotline and breaking policy by doing interviews with newspapers after training were taken by Wim alone. I have no doubt that he was taking advice from trusted confidants and I am sure he thought that any such advice was provided objectively and in his best interests. Sadly, I fear that the motivation of the advisers may have been very different.

We had played Hearts off the park in the three previous league encounters, although the results had been tight. There was a 2–1 victory at Tynecastle in October, followed by a victory at Celtic Park in December which was 1–0 going on 6–0. We then completely out-played them at Tynecastle, but referee Bobby Tait found enough stoppage time for Jose Quitongo to score an equaliser after 94 minutes

after we had missed a hatful of chances. It was a stuttering performance, though, at Celtic Park on 28 March, ending in an entirely
unsatisfactory 0–0 draw with two precious points lost and crunch
league matches against Kilmarnock and Rangers to follow.

It is never easy to win back-to-back Old Firm matches played within
a week of each other. So when we lost the cup semi-final I consoled
myself with the fact that history often showed that whoever lost the
first of two back-to-back matches frequently won the second. Bearing
in mind the fact that the league was the highest of our priorities, there
is no question which of the two I wanted to win more.

The signs were encouraging when we came from a goal behind at
Rugby Park on a dreadful wet evening to win the match against Kilmarnock by two goals to one, thanks to a splendid header from Henrik
Larsson and a delightful finish from Simon Donnelly. It certainly
looked as though we were back on the rails. It was not to be, however,
because the second of the Old Firm matches the following Sunday also
resulted in defeat, which gave a lifeline to Rangers in the league race
and cast a shadow of gloom over Celtic Park. This was the match in
which David Hannah came on as a late substitute for the injured Alan
Stubbs, then was himself replaced after we lost a goal, an incident
which had a shattering effect on David and upset his team-mates.

Back at the ground after the defeat at Ibrox, I was leaving the
stadium making for my car when I was approached by a group of
supporters who were, to say the least, thoroughly irate. They told me
that I would have to take serious action to resolve things in order to
make sure that the league was won. I asked if this meant that I should
interfere in the playing side – a comment I made with tongue heavily
in cheek, bearing in mind the press coverage – and I was told that this
was indeed my responsibility in circumstances where it looked as
though we might blow our league chances.

Despite these exhortations from the supporters, I can assure you
that I continued to perform my duty of non-interference in playing
matters. I remembered that our four closing matches in the league
were just about as attractive as you could hope for if you were in
contention. Our aim had always been to try to be in front of Rangers
and Hearts with these four matches left, three of them at home, against
Motherwell, Hibs and St Johnstone, and only one away, at East End
Park, Dunfermline.

The second defeat to Rangers meant that for the four-match run-in
the teams were absolutely level and there was a possibility that goal
difference could become crucial. A 4–1 victory against Motherwell

certainly helped the cause but a disappointing 0–0 draw at home against Hibs the following week kept the nerves jangling. Behind the scenes, in fact, we were immensely concerned that all the peripheral issues, particularly relating to the Wim Jansen position, were adversely affecting the challenge, although we had been given a lifeline by Rangers losing to Aberdeen.

Just about this time I had an intriguing interlude in the City Chambers with the Lord Provost of Glasgow, Mr Pat Lally, who was at the height of his troubles with the Labour Group trying to remove him from office. I had been attending a Celtic-sponsored event for young-sters with Harald Brattbakk, who managed to make a speech in English to a very substantial audience. The event had gone off very satisfac-torily and Harald and I were leaving with Peter McLean. On the way out of the building I walked straight into the Lord Provost, who was leaving his office. We had never met, but there was instant recognition thanks to media coverage. Accordingly, we walked over and greeted each other, with the Lord Provost saying to me, 'I am pleased to meet you – I have read all about you in the newspapers, although I don't believe a word of it!'

'Well, I've read all about you, too,' I replied. 'And I don't believe any of that either!'

With that, we laughed and shook hands warmly. It would have made a splendid picture in any of the newspapers!

On the penultimate weekend of the season our game was moved to the Sunday for television purposes and we received the best possible boost the day before when Gordon Marshall, who had been sold by us to Kilmarnock a short time earlier, performed heroics at Ibrox to earn a shut-out and an injury-time goal gave Kilmarnock victory. It meant that victory at Dunfermline would win the championship, and in view of the fact that we had beaten them four times since that shock home defeat in August, it looked as though the big moment was here. However, we appeared to settle on a one-goal lead at East End Park and were hanging on towards the end until, seven minutes from time, a looping header from Craig Faulconbridge shattered our dreams and left us still needing victory against St Johnstone in the last game six days later.

In the meantime, extensive research was being carried out in respect of Wim Jansen's successor. A number of candidates had been identified and detailed homework had been done. The issue was becoming clearer in terms of who should be targeted.

But the pressing priority for the week after the Dunfermline draw was the match against St Johnstone and, as far as the club was concerned, the immediate aftermath. If by any chance the championship was not won, the clear belief was that Wim Jansen would go and, either expressly or by implication, blame me for that failure. If it was won, he would accept all the adulation, announce his resignation, and I would take the blame. It was the classic no-win situation as far as I was concerned.

Believe it or not, one very close ally of mine suggested to me during that week that it would be better for Celtic not to win the championship on Saturday as far as my own position was concerned. I was utterly horrified and told him that even if I were to be strung up from the yardarm afterwards I would still virtually kill to win that championship. That was a genuine reaction and reflects the hold upon you that a club like Celtic can have after a very short period of time.

The problem for the club was how to manage the situation after the final match, win or lose. Wim Jansen was still to make his position clear and had indicated that he would do so immediately after the championship race was complete. There was also the matter of a game in Lisbon the following Tuesday evening as part of the Jorge Cadete transfer deal and no one knew whether or not Wim would be in charge for that match. The whole matter was considered carefully but once again the decision was taken – rightly, in my view – to do nothing until after the final match and then, to some extent, to allow Wim to set the agenda. One thing was clear – there would be no co-operation offered by the head coach in terms of planning.

I have never experienced and will never again experience the emotions of that final league match against St Johnstone. The atmosphere was utterly incredible, carrying a mixture of foreboding and anticipation. Anything other than victory could not be contemplated. I still shudder to think what might have happened had we lost that match 1–0. As it happened, Henrik Larsson eased the huge burden with a magnificent opening goal within three minutes and it looked then as though it might be party time. But when George O'Boyle headed just over from a wonderful opportunity before half-time, we had a clear reminder that it still wasn't over.

As the second half unfolded, tension developed again. No one had any doubt that Rangers would win at Tannadice against Dundee United. Even a draw was a disaster for Celtic. The tension clearly got to the players, and the performance level began to fall. Then, with fifteen minutes left, the captain Tom Boyd broke from defence (what an underestimated Celtic servant he has been). There followed a forty-yard run, a delightful chip into the path of Jackie McNamara, a splendid square pass and a finish of panache and conviction from Harald Brattbakk – and the roar of relief and celebration was chilling.

I was out of my seat. In the joy of the moment, even before I had sat back down, I realised what trauma lay ahead. The scenes of jubilation will never be forgotten. I looked on as the players took the acclaim of the supporters and as Wim Jansen savoured the moment before the cameras. Meanwhile, the real hero had slipped out of the directors' box and gone down the tunnel to the dug-out area to offer his congratulations immediately after the final whistle. He then shook hands with as many players as possible around the touchline and disappeared. Fergus McCann is not a man who likes the limelight. He believes celebrations in public are for players. Officials should stay in the background.

I then made my way down to the tunnel area, timing this with the arrival of Wim Jansen. As he walked up the tunnel I made towards him and said, 'Congratulations, well done.' He did not acknowledge me and cast his eyes firmly at the floor as he walked towards the dressing-room. A handshake was out of the question. For him to say later that I did not congratulate him was entirely out of order.

The edge was certainly taken off the winning of the championship by the total uncertainty over Wim Jansen's position at the club. After the match he again refused to indicate what his decision was. The media have accused me of arrogance on countless occasions. However, I can think of nothing more arrogant than the position adopted at that stage by the head coach.

Arrogance, incidentally, according to the Oxford dictionary, is defined as 'aggressively assertive' or 'presumptuous'. I would put the arrogance demonstrated by Wim Jansen as he kept everyone waiting for his decision in the 'presumptuous' category. As far as my own 'arrogance' is concerned, I still prefer to leave others to form views and make judgements, so long as these are fair and objective. In fairness, I can understand why the adjective could have been used to describe me on certain occasions because I know that my tolerance level was not high, especially when I was consistently facing loaded questioning which was frequently based on totally erroneous and often mischievous foundations.

But, for the moment, the spotlight was on Wim. Not even the winning of the championship could deflect completely from the circus he had created by his utterances six weeks earlier. All the club officials could do was sit and wait, because they were certainly not given the privilege of being party to the situation by Wim.

I had mixed feelings about whether or not an announcement should be made that night. Obviously, if he had indicated, as I was sure he was going to do, that he was leaving, then that would have detracted massively from the occasion and I did believe the supporters were entitled to at least one night's unfettered celebration after ten years of championship famine. But the uncertainty had to be removed, and the sooner the better. My research into a potential successor had moved on apace and I was certainly in a position to start making concrete moves as soon as Wim spoke up. All I needed was the go-ahead from the board.

My total elation at our championship success was instantly tempered by the troubled times which I knew were around the corner. I had no doubt Wim was leaving, even less doubt that I would carry the can. It also meant that the pleasant summer I had initially anticipated was out of the question because of the need to move for a head coach and then on player transfers. While for Wim the task had been completed, for me the work was just beginning.

Around eight o'clock I made my way home, mightily relieved in one sense and severely troubled in another. I could sense what was ahead. There was no question of going out to celebrate. It was now a time for quiet contemplation.

The next day the squad had to travel to Portugal for the Jorge Cadete match against Sporting Lisbon on the Tuesday evening. It had already been established that neither Fergus nor I would travel so that we could continue our efforts in respect of the inevitable replacement required for the head coach.

On the Monday morning Fergus and I were locked in discussions on this subject when we received news from Lisbon. We had anticipated that Wim would make his announcement after the party returned from Portugal. We did not expect him to make an announcement while away with the team.

The news we received was that he had told the directors on site in Lisbon that he was making an announcement that day to the effect that he was leaving. He intended to tell the players at 1.30 p.m. and hold a press conference at 4 p.m. At that, public relations manager Peter McLean was brought in and he apparently attempted to reach some agreement with Wim about the handling of the situation now that his decision was to be made public. He was asked, indeed, why he had decided to make the announcement that day. The reply was that his wife was running Henrik Larsson from his home to Glasgow Airport that day since he had been excused travelling because of international commitments for Sweden. Wim had authorised his wife to tell Henrik of his decision and that would be happening around lunchtime. In these circumstances, he said, it was vital that he tell the other players around the same time.

It became clear instantly that there would be no co-operation with regard to the manner in which he announced his departure. He made it clear that he would do things his way and would say whatever he thought fit to the players and the media. He did not tell anyone what he intended to do or say, especially at the press conference at four o'clock, which meant that Fergus and I were left in Glasgow completely in the dark as to his intentions.

By virtue of the fact that Wim was not willing to provide any co-operation at all with the officials in Lisbon, it was clear to us that we could anticipate the worst in that he would go with a volley directed towards me and, probably, Fergus. We decided to prepare on that basis, although we kept the position open by calling a press conference for 5 p.m. in Glasgow. That hour was very important. We arranged for a call to be made to us at around 4.45 p.m. to advise us of the line taken by Wim so that we could finalise the line we should take before the press in Scotland.

Had Wim said that he had always wanted to be in Glasgow only for one year, had enjoyed the year very much but felt it was now time for him to move on to another challenge, we would simply have regretted his decision and wished him well. However, our worst fears were confirmed. He went out with guns blazing in Lisbon, attacking me in particular. That was exactly what we expected and what we had been prepared to handle.

I understand that the position in Lisbon was exacerbated by one journalist who started a question to Wim by saying that Jock Brown had let it be known that he believed Wim had been tapped by Liverpool. Apparently he lost the place at that. It is the oldest trick in the book. I had never 'let it be known' that I believed he had been tapped by Liverpool or by anyone else. Indeed, I had expressed this opinion in the clearest possible way to the directors. At the time of the press conference in Glasgow I did not know that that point had been put to Wim in Lisbon, yet when I was asked the question about any possible tapping of our head coach I indicated unequivocally that I was sure that had not taken place.

It was a field day for the media. Fergus had prepared a full statement in relation to Wim's decision, as follows:

First and foremost, this period of time is about Celtic winning the league championship and the supporters and players deserve to celebrate.

As for Wim Jansen, he originally wanted a one-year contract. The club agreed a three-year term, with the option for both sides to terminate the contract after one year. This was one of the key elements of the agreement, as well as a commitment to keep its content confidential.

Wim has decided to leave after one year as Celtic's head coach. The club accepts Wim's decision, which is not unexpected.

The decision Wim has taken is one that the board also believes is best for the club. On behalf of everyone at Celtic, I would like to thank Wim for his time at the club and wish him all the best for the future.

The supporters should not let Wim's decision deflect their attention and pleasure from the point that the league has been won. They deserve to celebrate. Wim has played a part and no one should deny that but so have many others. The players deserve a large slice of the credit, as do the supporters who have made the dream become reality. They have provided the personal and financial backing to build a team and stadium that every Celtic supporter has a right to be proud of and stayed behind the team week after week, year after year.

As for the future, there are exciting times ahead and in August we will have a full Celtic Park to celebrate the flag coming home.

The nature of football now sees players and coaches changing clubs more frequently than in the past. We must all accept and embrace change as an exciting challenge and ensure that it also results in progress.

Celtic has risen through adversity and become stronger and stronger every season for the last four years. I have no doubt this will continue next season as the club moves onwards and upwards.

Many people told Celtic that it was wrong to appoint a new coach this time last year. In July 1997 headlines and hotlines screamed criticism at the appointment of Wim Jansen but, despite all the noise, Celtic has kept its eye on the ball, the League and League Cup have been won, a 60,000-seat stadium will host 50,000 season-ticket holders and the scene is set for the next exciting stage in Celtic's history.

Finally, I want to emphasise an important point: all of this was not the result of the efforts of only one season or of one man. I want to pay tribute to all those at the club, especially the players, all of whom have worked so hard for success, some for four years or more.

Individuals will always come and go but the legend that is Celtic continues.

Fergus McCann does not issue press statements without very careful thought. The sentence which caught the imagination of the media was 'The decision Wim has taken is one that the board also believes is best for the club'. He knew that he would be bombarded by questions about that sentence. That eventually resulted in headlines screaming that Fergus had said Wim would be sacked anyway. He did not say that.

The reason for his observation was that it had become abundantly clear that Wim had no interest whatsoever in co-operating with the board of directors in relation to the way in which the club was to be run. He had ignored the club policy about watching players live before spending a significant sum of money in the case of Harald Brattbakk, and he had point-blank refused to co-operate in the necessary preparatory work involved in bringing in new players for the season ahead. That kind of co-operation was essential from any head coach and if it was refused by the person holding down the post, it was obviously preferable that he should move on.

What Fergus said was that for Wim to continue in his post there would have had to have been changes in terms of his implementing of club policy. He would have had to have agreed to the policy of watching players live before significant spending and he would have had to have provided the necessary information to enable the club to put together budgets to finance his playing-staff requirements. In short, he would have had to have been prepared to implement policies laid down by the board. The indication he had given at the time of his appointment was that he would do so, but that had not turned out to be the case.

Fergus was then asked what the position would have been had Wim refused to co-operate with club policy. When Fergus indicated that it would have been extremely difficult for him to remain in the post, that was translated as meaning that he would have been sacked anyway and that was how the matter was reported.

The accurate position was that had Wim sat down with the board of directors and confirmed that, notwithstanding the actions of the past months, he would now implement their policies in full and would provide the necessary level of co-operation to the management of the club, then obviously he could have continued in his post. We all knew, however, that there was no way such co-operation would be forthcoming.

At that press conference, I also had to defend myself against the criticism levelled at me in Lisbon by Wim. I was supposed to be hard to work with and to have been unwilling to pursue transfer targets, not at all in some cases and too slowly in others. I do not recall anyone asking me if I had found Wim difficult to work with. The answer would have been, 'Yes, virtually impossible.'

The irony was that I was receiving such criticism after five months of blatant appeasement on my part. Think about it. The board of directors laid down a policy for me to implement, including the manner in which I was to deal with the head coach. I found these instructions totally acceptable and tried to carry them out to the best of my ability. I was met with regular obstruction which I then had to explain to the directors, to whom I had to report on a regular basis, frequently in writing.

Similarly, I was the one who had to present a coherent proposal in respect of any player Wim sought to bring to the club. Names were cast up to me at that press conference, Wim having claimed that I had refused to pursue his interest in certain high-profile players. Apparently I had delayed in pursuing Karlheinz Riedle from Borussia Dortmund. I had not pursued Les Ferdinand, who had moved from Newcastle United to Tottenham Hotspur.

In relation to Riedle, the truth was that in a chin-stroking session of bandying names around early in the season, his name had been mentioned. As usual, I asked questions, most of which were not received happily. I made the point that he was around thirty-two years old and had just appeared in the European Cup-winning team for Borussia Dortmund. I asked if anyone knew why in these circumstances they were prepared to release him while he was still under contract. Was there any chance that his legs had gone? Had anyone seen him play recently? Should someone not go and see him play now? There was never any doubt that he was a top-class player but he would obviously represent a very substantial investment without any real prospect of there being a return on the money spent.

I remember making enquiries about the likely price and wage demands and suggested that Davie Hay, who was still on board at the time, should go and see him play to ensure that his fitness level was still acceptable. I duly found out the transfer fee requested and his salary requirements. Both were extremely substantial. In the meantime, no one went to see him play. Suddenly, he signed for Liverpool.

When Ferdinand was mentioned, I knew that his asking price was £6 million and that he, too, was in the region of 32 years old and would require a very substantial financial package to attract him to Glasgow. Was that the best possible use of our resources? I do not recall a response.

Throughout the season there was only one player for whom a good detailed case was presented and who was pursued unsuccessfully. We failed only because his club would not sell him at any price, even an inflated one. All other targets for whom a case was coherently made were duly brought to the club.

There was also a consistent request for Pierre Van Hooijdonk. I carried out detailed enquiries into the Van Hooijdonk position at Celtic and then advised Wim that in the light of these enquiries, which had nothing to do with his technical qualities, it was impossible to make a case to the board for his repurchase. I did have one very frank exchange with Wim before the policy of appeasement started, at a point when he was blaming me for not having Paolo Di Canio, Jorge Cadete and Pierre Van Hooijdonk in the ranks. All three had already left the club when he mentioned their names once too often and I indicated to him that I wanted to reach an agreement there and then that their names would never again be mentioned by him in my presence.

Anyway, by Tuesday, 12 May, the fact that Celtic had won the championship had been submerged in miles of column inches relating to the Jansen departure. Suddenly the man who originally would not give the press the time of day became garrulous in the extreme when faced by a journalist or a microphone. Apparently he flipped totally when he was told in Portugal the oversimplified version of what Fergus had said about the difficulty in him remaining in the job, and wonderful media fodder poured out of him all that week, including at a press conference arranged for him by the club in a Glasgow hotel on the Friday.

The policy taken by me at that time was only to respond to things he said. As soon as he chose to be quiet then I would too. Even then, I was totally unhappy about being dragged into any defence of myself or attack upon him. From the point when the team arrived back in Glasgow on the Wednesday to Wim's last visit to Celtic Park on the Friday, there was no contact between us. All the formalities were taken care of by Eric Riley, in his capacity as finance director, and there appeared to be no merit whatsoever in attempting any level of communication.

In any event, I was already heavily embroiled in pursuing the man who had become the club's prime target to take over as head coach and I was preparing once again to use my passport.

CHAPTER 15

The Man from Norway

In the midst of the fall-out over Wim Jansen's departure, another insidious story appeared in the press accusing me once again of being arrogant and of having so little regard for Craig Burley's capacity to make a speech at the Scottish Football Writers' Association Dinner that I had handed him a speech, unsolicited, for use when he received his Player of the Year award. Once again, it appeared in print, therefore it must be true. That is the sad conclusion reached by so many readers uninitiated in the workings of some sections of the press.

The truth was that Craig had revealed to me prior to the dinner that he was very nervous indeed about having to make a speech and in the course of that conversation I had told him that if he wanted any ideas or assistance I would be happy to help. He accepted willingly and asked if I could give him some material. I had attended that particular dinner on a regular basis and had, sadly, seen one or two thoroughly deserving recipients let themselves down very badly when it came to making the acceptance speech.

Accordingly, I prepared one and a half pages of material for Craig's consideration. When I gave it to him he protested that it was too long! I made it clear that this was only a suggestion and he could do with the material exactly as he pleased. As it turned out, he did not use the material and handled things his own way. This was perfectly in order as far as I was concerned and if my suggestions helped his thought process then I am delighted. I certainly did not see his failure to use the material offered as any kind of slight. I only heard second hand what he did actually say at the dinner because, surprise, surprise, I did not receive an invitation! What is clear, however, is that the nastily distorted version of events which appeared in the tabloid newspaper was completely unjustified.

By the time Wim Jansen was packing his bags and leaving Celtic Park as head coach for the last time, the identity of our potential new head coach had been established.

All the homework which could possibly have been done without actually speaking to a candidate had been carried out in the most painstaking fashion. The result was that the man we wanted to speak to was Egil Olsen, the Norwegian national manager who was preparing his team for the World Cup finals in France. His record as Norway's manager was truly remarkable and while he had attracted criticism because of what was believed to be a 'long-ball policy', everything pointed to him being a winner with a very clear vision for success and focused commitment.

Since it was obviously very important for the new head coach to be on a similar wavelength to those already at Celtic and to understand what the club was trying to achieve, I was despatched as the advance party to conduct the initial interview in Oslo. Olsen came over as a shy, reserved man who came alive when he talked about football and was clearly totally immersed in his profession. We talked for a couple of hours and we could have gone on for another couple. I challenged him about the long-ball allegation and he explained in substantial detail his philosophy on the game and the methods which he believed were most likely to bring success to any team. He was very impressive indeed. That enabled me to report back to the directors in a favourable light and an arrangement was made for him to meet several board members in London a few days later. That interview took place outwith my presence, quite properly, although I was there to introduce the parties.

Just as the pursuit of Egil Olsen was hotting up in the middle of May, Murdo MacLeod arrived at Celtic Park looking to see me.

'What's happening?' he asked. 'What are the club's plans with regard to a new head coach?'

I told him that the matter was now under serious consideration following the eventual announcement by Wim Jansen but I was not in a position to tell him anything at that time.

'I would like to put my hat in the ring for the job,' he said.

'Do you think you are ready to take on such a job?' I replied.

He assured me that he certainly believed that he was capable of doing the job and would love to be given the chance. When I asked him if he was effectively making a formal application to be considered as one of the candidates, he replied that he most certainly wanted to be considered as a candidate. I told him I would report the position to the board.

During the conversation I did remind him that when he had first come on board as assistant head coach I had indicated to him that I thought he could become a serious candidate for the post only after

Wim had served his three-year contract. I did feel that after only one year the chances of him being offered the top job were not good. To be perfectly honest, I found myself in some difficulty here in that I had no doubt whatsoever that his chances were nil. However, it was certainly not for me to do other than prepare him gently for the likelihood of being unsuccessful in his application, rather than say absolutely nothing and hide behind a board decision.

I regarded his appointment to the club the previous summer as the biggest mistake I had made during my entire period at Celtic and I knew that my recommendation to the board would be that he should not remain in place when a new head coach arrived. However, I still thought it only fair that he should be given an opportunity to state his case so that I could relay this to the board.

I reminded him that the club had not been entirely satisfied with *all* aspects of Wim Jansen's stewardship of the club and that he had allied himself totally to the head coach. It was important for the board to know whether or not in appointing Murdo they could expect more of the same.

Murdo leapt on that immediately. 'I understand that,' he said. 'I would be my own man. There were aspects of Wim's coaching that I did not agree with and I would certainly be making changes if I were given the job.'

I asked for clarification of the areas in which he differed from Wim so far as handling the team was concerned and he immediately identified two areas.

'I would do much more work on set pieces. I also did not agree with Wim's policy on the use of substitutes.'

In both instances Murdo would have been aware of disquiet felt on these two topics within the club. I was aware from players that there was no work done on attacking set pieces in training and I had asked Murdo at one point during the season to confirm if this was correct. He had done so.

The point about set pieces was a very interesting one. It is routine for professional clubs to rehearse set pieces and to work out moves to try to take the opposition by surprise. During the whole of the 1997–98 season I can recall the team scoring only once from a free kick, a curling 25-yarder from Henrik Larsson at Celtic Park against Aberdeen, and only about three times from corner kicks, one from Malky Mackay at Easter Road in the opening league match and others from Morten Wieghorst and Craig Burley – and I can recall none being the result of obvious rehearsed play. Apparently, Wim's attitude was that since every game was covered by television, rehearsing moves was counter-productive. He preferred to leave it to the initiative and ingenuity of the players on the pitch at the time to come up with set-piece ploys.

It was also often the case that substitutes were not introduced at all or were introduced very late by Wim. This had been commented upon in many quarters but again it appeared to be an area in which Murdo did not agree with his head coach.

In fairness to Murdo, there was obviously a very good case technically for his observations on both counts. However, I admit that I was already conditioned by our discussion the previous October in which Murdo had indicated that he could be one hundred per cent more supportive if he had a better deal. As the ally who had helped him out of his Dumbarton contract and negotiated his Partick Thistle one before receiving several phone calls seeking my assistance after he had left Partick Thistle, I had now been told what was really required in order to obtain appropriate support.

I would further admit that following that meeting in October 1997, supported by the manner in which Murdo had conducted himself in the job before, during and after that time, I was no longer of a mind to hang my hat on Murdo's implementation of his particular definition of loyalty.

Murdo was disappearing on holiday for two weeks and I told him that I would contact him if there were any relevant matters to discuss, failing which I would see him on his return. I concluded by indicating that I did not think he had a realistic chance of being offered the number-one post, although I would convey the terms of our discussion to the directors. During that fortnight I hoped that the club would finalise its dealings and make an appointment.

Following my initial satisfactory meeting with Egil Olsen and his lengthy discussion with the board, the decision was taken to try to pin him down to a contract which would hopefully be announced prior to the World Cup. However, it was also important for his wife to be happy about the move, and as a result we arranged to fly her from Oslo to Glasgow to have a look around the city and at possible places to live. She duly arrived with a close friend and I arranged for her to be shown around. I even joined her for lunch in the Walfrid Restaurant. She expressed herself as very happy with what she had seen. She had a close interest in football and was accordingly intrigued to see the stadium. Her only concern was the fact that the family dog would have to go into quarantine.

Everything appeared positive, so much so that I attended a meeting with the executive of the Celtic Supporters' Association to give them a briefing on the current state of play. I indicated to them that we had identified the man we wanted as head coach, were involved in negotiations and were very optimistic that we had our man. That, interestingly enough, was later attributed to me as a lie by members of the Supporters' Association even though it was most certainly entirely accurate at the time.

Indeed, I underplayed the position with the executive a little in order to be cautious. By the time I met them, terms had been established in principle through Olsen's agents and the main issue appeared to be when he could start work and when the appointment could be announced. He remained reluctant to have any announce-ment made prior to the World Cup, whereas we were most anxious to make that announcement at the earliest opportunity. He was also concerned about the fact that he had a hip replacement operation planned and would require time off to recover. He had already been subjected to a hip-replacement operation some years before but it had to be done again and would need to be carried out during the coming season. I assured him that this would not be a difficulty for the club.

The last weekend in May I was scheduled to be attending a supporters' function in New York. The invitation had been extended several weeks earlier and I had been very happy to accept. Indeed, I had made an arrangement to go on holiday immediately after that trip to America. I was completely confident that by that time the head coach would have been appointed and the necessary work carried out. Instead I spent that weekend in Oslo meeting Egil Olsen once again to attempt to finalise all the details of his arrival in Glasgow and to persuade him to allow the announcement to be made prior to his meeting up with his players for the World Cup within the next week.

An apology for absence had to be made to the supporters' club in New York but when it was explained to them by Fergus McCann that I had had to withdraw because of pressing business relating to the appointment of a head coach, they readily understood and could not have been more pleasant. But that did not stop the *Daily Record* carrying a story to the effect that the supporters in New York had withdrawn my invitation. They were so incensed on the other side of the Atlantic by this press report that they insisted upon an apology being printed by the newspaper. A correction was issued to the effect that there had been no withdrawal of any invitation and I had called off for good reasons.

I was picked up at Oslo Airport by Mrs Olsen and taken to their house overlooking the city. Once again I found Egil to be charming and a very impressive individual. By the time he dropped me back at the airport in Oslo for the return journey it had been established that he was coming to Celtic Park but he was still very unhappy about any announcement being made prior to the World Cup. He indicated that he would consider the matter very carefully with his advisers and revert to me. The only real point of discussion at this time was when the announcement would be made. I haven't spoken to him since.

There followed countless discussions with his advisers. Terms were agreed, but it was eventually conveyed to us that Olsen would not entertain any announcement being made until after Norway's interest in the World Cup was over. We agreed to co-operate with that, albeit reluctantly. However, we wanted unequivocal confirmation that he would be coming to Celtic Park and some detail of proposed timing. Suddenly, even his advisers could not obtain any answers from him. While he was in France with the Norwegian squad I initially spoke to the agents involved on a daily basis, but they could not apparently obtain any clear answers from him about when the contract could be signed and when he would arrive in Glasgow. I started to become extremely nervous. Time was passing and the matter was not finalised the way it should have been.

I knew he was completely committed to Norway's World Cup campaign and understood that. However, I could not understand the failure of his advisers to obtain clear answers to reassure us that everything was in order. The only message I could get from them was that there would be no further discussion with him until Norway were out of the World Cup. I realised then that if there were to be any problems, we would be leaving it much too late to consider other options. It was on that basis that we reverted to our list of potential candidates and set up the possibility of an alternative.

One of the names on the list at that time was Gerard Houllier. I made initial contact with him and then met up with him. At that first discussion I indicated to him that we were clearly focused on who we thought would become our new head coach but I wanted to establish his position in the event that the vacancy remained available.

Houllier is a charming individual. I spent a lot of time with him, including a very lengthy lunch in Paris followed by a visit to his home, and I like him enormously. His coaching credentials are also excellent. However, he made it clear to me from the start that he had been approached by Liverpool. That was where his heart lay, since he had spent a lot of time there in his youth, and he expected everything to be tidied up as soon as his involvement in the World Cup was over. He was heavily involved with both FIFA and the French Federation.

With Houllier effectively out of the picture, I was receptive when the name Dr Jozef Venglos emerged from one of my trips to France. He was on duty as a member of the FIFA Technical Committee and was heavily involved in the analysis of the World Cup. My principal knowledge of him related to his spell as manager of Aston Villa in the 1990–91 season. On the face of it that had not turned out to be an immensely successful period, but when I made more detailed enquiries I discovered that this was a gross oversimplification of what had happened. His standing there remained extremely high. He had won a Manager of the Month award early in his time at Villa Park and had then been compelled to sell David Platt for financial reasons. I also discovered that he had been a trailblazer for foreign coaches in the United Kingdom and had faced a very difficult time. Hardly any other manager in English football at that time was other than British and there had been a negative reaction to the intrusion of a foreigner.

In a nutshell, the information which emerged was that Jozef Venglos had been well ahead of his time at Aston Villa and had gone there at a time when British football had not been ready for the Continental approach. Obviously, times had now changed.

Before attempting to arrange to see Jozef I conducted very detailed enquiries and everywhere I turned the reaction was positive. He was clearly held in the highest regard by coaches all over the world, and when I expressed concern about his advancing years, I was constantly assured that he was among the most modern of coaches and that his unbridled enthusiasm for the game had ensured that he had kept up with all the modern trends. Indeed, he was credited with leading many of the new trends in world football.

I reported to Fergus McCann on the enquiries I had made and sought authority to arrange to meet Jozef in person for preliminary talks. That authority was forthcoming and I was able to move to the next stage.

But during this time Murdo MacLeod's summer holiday had come to an end. He arrived unannounced in my office at the beginning of June to find out what was happening and what his position was in the context of the head coach vacancy. His position had, of course, been determined during his absence following his earlier meeting with me. The decision reached was that he would not be appointed head coach and, indeed, that his continuation as assistant head coach was not appropriate. The feeling was that it would not be right to impose him on Wim's successor. Neither I nor the directors could readily forget 'I could be one hundred per cent more supportive of you if I had a better deal'. He had, in fact, clearly established that without the better deal the support which the club should have received was not available.

A decision had therefore been taken that the time had come for Murdo to part company with the club and I saw no basis for delaying telling him this. I did so in a painstaking, detailed fashion and detected instantly his change of demeanour and tone. I told him that he had been unsuccessful in his application for the post as head coach and that the news was in fact worse in that it had been decided that he should not continue as assistant head coach either. A conversation like that is never easy. Ideally it would have taken place with some notice and preferably with a board member present. However, Murdo's sudden arrival earlier than I anticipated had left me in an awkward position.

I made it clear that I would co-operate in every way in terms of the manner of his departure and had no intention of becoming involved in any detailed public explanation. I also explained to him that it would have been extremely easy for me to have waited until the new head coach had been appointed and then effectively blamed that new head coach for Murdo's departure. That would have been a dereliction of my responsibility and a distortion of the facts. On that basis I felt it essential to look him in the eye and tell him that his time at the club was over.

It would, indeed, have been very easy to have kept him on board until the new head coach arrived. No one would have blinked if the new man had been appointed and Murdo had departed. That is seen to be a routine procedure in the world of football today. However, it would have been unfair to hide behind a new head coach in such a decision-making process, and it was also very important to be able to say to the new man that the field was clear for him to make an appointment without being compelled to deal immediately with the issue of his predecessor's right-hand man.

Murdo was not a happy man. He insisted that the players would be furious to find that he was leaving the club. I knew that to be entirely wrong. Indeed, one player said to me after his departure that many of the players had been concerned that he might remain in place at the elbow of the new head coach. I did not enquire as to the basis for these observations but certainly obtained the clear understanding that, for a substantial number of the players at least, Murdo's departure would present no difficulty.

Obviously, during the course of the meeting, at which Murdo appeared genuinely surprised to have his contract terminated, I considered it reasonable for him to have some time to consider his position and said he should revert to me the following day to agree the presentation to the public of his departure from the club. Even as I was discussing this with him, I detected a suggestion that he would not go quietly and that there was trouble ahead.

Any doubts I had were eliminated as soon as he arrived at Celtic Park the following morning to make it clear that he would be doing his own thing in relation to his departure and that I could do whatever I saw fit on behalf of the club. That discussion was apparently part of the stirring-up process for the tabloid disclosures to follow. I knew then precisely what was coming. Indeed, following Murdo's final departure that Thursday, I reported to the directors not only that he had gone but that we could read his version of events in the *Sunday Mail* that weekend. At that point I had discussions with our public relations manager, Peter McLean, to try to pre-empt the publicity we could expect on the Sunday. I was very anxious to call a press conference on the Saturday involving every Sunday news-paper except the *Sunday Mail* at which the club's position could be clearly established.

Obviously, there was concern on Peter's part that I might be wrong in my assessment that Murdo would be selling his story to the *Sunday Mail* and I had to confess that this was simply my reading of the situation. I had no hard facts to back up the theory. But these hard facts were made available on the Saturday morning when radio advertisements presented the usual 'Read my story in tomorrow's *Sunday Mail*'. Once again I contacted Peter McLean and pushed very hard for a press conference to take place that afternoon as I had originally wanted. Peter correctly felt that this should be canvassed around members of the board and he took it upon himself to make the necessary phone calls. Fergus was, in fact, on holiday at the time and not contactable.

After Peter's trawl around the directors, he reported back to me that the overall view was that we should say nothing and wait to see what Murdo said before considering any reaction. They did not want any tit-for-tat information flying around, nor did we want to wash our dirty linen in public. I sympathised with that position. However, there are times when I think it is necessary to be proactive in respect of putting out the club's position, rather than reactive. But I had been overruled and as an employee of the club I could not challenge or overturn a decision made by the directors. Accordingly, I simply had to wait until Sunday and accept the inevitable assault.

Murdo stooped to depths which surprised even someone who had become totally disenchanted with his *modus operandi*. He and the *Sunday Mail* knew exactly what buttons to press. 'Jock Wanted To Pick The Team!' the headline blasted. As is so frequently the case, the actual content of the article barely sustained the headline, but you could imagine every Celtic supporter in the country choking over his cornflakes when he digested that particular piece of nonsense.

The daily newspapers couldn't wait to follow up on the Sunday piece. Once again I was anxious to hold a press conference to give the club's side of the story, albeit one day late as far as I was concerned. Once again I was thwarted in this. Peter McLean took soundings from directors and yet again the decision was taken that we should not become involved and should retain a dignified silence. While I was convinced that this was the wrong decision, I always bowed completely to decisions made on matters in which I had a personal involvement. It seemed appropriate to trust the objectivity of colleagues in such circumstances and I still believe that this is the correct course of action. I never doubted the good faith of the decision taken above me.

However, hindsight established that this again was a bad decision. My great concern was that only one agenda was out there in the market place at the time. If the daily papers received nothing from the club then the only agenda in the market place on the Monday was still Murdo's. My feeling was that if I had taken the opportunity that Sunday to spell out the club's position on the matter, the daily newspapers would at least have been split on their attitude to the material which had been sold to the *Sunday Mail*. As it was, without any comment from me on behalf of the club, they perpetuated the only agenda they had any knowledge of – Murdo's.

By the Monday morning it was apparent that the club could no longer remain silent. The damage was extensive. It was unrealistic to expect any daily newspaper to attack the distorted MacLeod version of events when they did not have any other version to consider. The decision of the directors on the Monday was that it was necessary to speak up, and accordingly a press conference was called. I did have the opportunity to attack the nonsense spouted by Murdo. But it really was too late. The initiative had been lost, and while the papers did report what I had said in response, two days of unfettered publicity of a totally negative kind were too big a handicap.

Imagine if we had held a press conference on the Saturday. All those papers excluded from Murdo's 'revelations' would have heard the club's position and would have had the opportunity to write simultaneously on the Sunday. Our supporters would have had the opportunity at that point to form a view from both versions, Murdo's nonsense and the correct one. That opportunity was lost, and while the attempted redemption on the Monday helped, it could not wipe out the impact the two clear days' advantage had had.

In fairness to Murdo, I do not think even he would have anticipated the other fall-out from his payday. Two separate and unconnected death threats were made which, by their nature, required to be taken seriously by the club and me, and also by the police. They appeared to be as a direct result of material sold to the *Sunday Mail* by Murdo.

The following Sunday another mystery appeared to be solved. The heading was 'Smug Jock Wanted To Take Credit For Cup Win'. The story went on to detail my anxiety to carry the trophy off the bus at Celtic Park after returning from winning the Coca-Cola Cup the previous November. Now I wonder what anonymous source had fed that nonsense to newspapers some months before?

I am always intrigued at how some newspapers frequently manage to put in an offensive adjective like 'smug' when pieces like that are written. These are words over which it is impossible to take legal action and which are designed to leave an impression with the reader consistent with the wishes of the publication or the paid contributor.

By this time, though, the impact was infinitely less and it looked as though the unhappy experience of having worked with Murdo MacLeod could be confined to history. It would have been, but for his unedifying appearances on European trips, at Celtic Park, at the team's pre-match hotel and on radio and television pontificating about all things Celtic.

One very significant fact is incontrovertible, especially when considering the merit in his plea for a bigger salary: Murdo MacLeod has been available to take up any position in Scottish football without compensation since June 1997. In that time every club currently in the Premier Division except Hearts and Kilmarnock has changed manager. In the case of Aberdeen and Motherwell, this has happened twice. Add to that clubs like Hibernian and St Mirren, who have also changed manager in that period, and it seems fair to wonder why Murdo MacLeod has not been hired.

But while that regrettable sideshow was ongoing, a much more important issue still needed to be resolved – the appointment of a new head coach.

CHAPTER 16

Welcome, Dr Venglos

The search for the new head coach had taken another twist. Mr Z, who had ruled himself out by virtue of a contractual situation set up in April, reappeared on the scene. There were problems in connection with his new post and he retained a very strong interest in coming to Glasgow, if the job was still available.

As usual, the matter was extremely complicated. For me it meant urgent flights to London and then on to Europe to pursue the matter as carefully as I could, in order to establish whether or not Mr Z might yet be a possibility. Considerable dialogue took place with Mr Z and representatives on his behalf. It steadily became clear that in order for him to become a candidate he would have to break his word and deal with a potential breach of contract. Such was the man's integrity that when all that became established he indicated to me that, much as he would love to have come to Celtic, he could not do so in the particular circumstances.

Simultaneously, I had established that Jozef Venglos was interested. I talked to him on the telephone and then arranged a lengthy meeting in Vienna. He was extremely impressive and I could understand readily why he had immense stature in world football.

In a lifetime of consuming interest in football I have never known anyone whose high reputation as a football coach was more than matched by his standing as a human being. It became eerie. Throughout all my research, no one had a critical word for Jozef Venglos. There was nothing but praise, admiration and respect. I returned from Vienna and reported appropriately to Fergus with the strong recommendation that a meeting should be arranged with directors with a view to appointing him. Such a meeting was duly convened and the outcome was that Jozef Venglos should be our man.

As you can imagine, however, nothing is ever simple. A work permit was required. Along with the club's solicitors I embarked urgently on all the formalities with a view to bringing Jozef to Glasgow as soon after the World Cup finals as possible, bearing in mind that our first match was scheduled to take place on 18 July at Rugby Park, Kilmarnock, a testimonial match for Ray Montgomerie.

In the meantime, Jozef bled me dry for information about Celtic and the set-up. He was fully acquainted with all the international players in our squad and asked for a full run-down on all other first-team squad members.

He wanted details of our youth development system and of our coaching staff. He wanted to know all about the medical back-up, the fitness training and the policies for looking after all the players, from the most senior to the youngest.

I had already explained to Jozef that pre-season training was being handled by Eric Black, Danny McGrain and Kenny McDowall, with Eric and Kenny in charge of the pre-season trip to Holland for training purposes. It was made clear to him that he would have total power over selecting a right-hand man, but he indicated that he wanted to disrupt existing coaching staff as little as possible and would attempt to work with them as far as he could before contemplating any new recruits. He also made it clear, just as Wim Jansen had done, that he preferred the idea of a Scottish right-hand man to keep him fully abreast of the lie of the land.

Among the plethora of names being canvassed in the media for the job, the name of Jozef Venglos never cropped up. The smart money was going on Gerard Houllier, since the earlier 'informed' tips about men like David Jones of Southampton and Martin O'Neill of Leicester City had petered out. It never ceases to amaze me how names crop up. It is certainly true that I spoke to Gerard Houllier. Poor David Jones was put in a position of having to make some comment from Southampton, and his chairman was also compelled to deal with press enquiries. Yet, fine manager though he no doubt is, neither he nor Martin O'Neill was ever the subject of any discussion to which I was party. Neither fitted the criteria established by the board, which I was, of course, obliged to observe

Immediately after the World Cup final on 12 July, we moved with the utmost alacrity to try to have Jozef Venglos on duty prior to the match against Kilmarnock on 18 July. We were quickly made aware of the fact that the work permit could not be cleared in that timescale but that the applications had to be lodged and checked with the Department for Education and Employment, whose officials were, I have to say, immensely helpful.

On the basis that the documentation was in order, we earmarked Thursday, 16 July, as the announcement date, but that then had to be delayed 24 hours because of the paperwork involved. That brought about the announcement of Gerard Houllier as manager of Liverpool on 16 July, my ridiculing in many areas of the media on the morning of 17 July and the appointment of Jozef on the same date, subject to his being granted a work permit.

On the afternoon of 16 July a rumour apparently spread around Glasgow that I had resigned. The club was forced to issue a statement to the effect that this was nonsense. Nevertheless, the 'failure to bring in Houllier' in the eyes of some sections of the media resulted even in essentially decent journalists like Stewart Weir of the Scottish *Mirror* writing an article noting the denial of my resignation and saying 'Why not?'.

The bottom line was that no one in the media was aware of our interest in Jozef Venglos and no one had any idea at all that his appointment was to be announced the day the headlines screamed for my head for failing to get Houllier. The effect of that was that when Jozef Venglos was announced as the new head coach on Friday, 17 July, the reception was largely negative. One newspaper even attacked Jozef by saying that he had not coached a club since 1993. The same newspaper had extolled the virtues of Gerard Houllier for the post, without mentioning the fact that he had not coached a club side since 1986! 'Dr Who?' the headlines screamed. It wasn't so much, in my opinion, the press attacking Jozef. It was more an expression of frustration and anger at the fact that the journalists had not had a clue that he was in the offing.

There is a lesson to be learned, of course. If you want to have something well received by the public, leak it to the media first so that it appears to be their idea and thus gets a warm reception. That's a game which is played frequently within the world of football, but not by Celtic under Fergus McCann. That does not sit easily with club policy.

So on Saturday, 18 July, our supporters had been told by many sections of the media that they should not be particularly happy with the appointment of Jozef Venglos. They should also be highly critical of me for taking so long to bring in a new head coach. Forget the background and the complexities. Forget the fact that the power vested in me by the press was imaginary, in that I could not appoint any head coach but could only do the homework and recommend names in line with the policy clearly set out by the board of directors. I took instructions from, and reported to, that board. Forget all that. Simply pillory Brown and cast aspersions on the man deemed to be his choice, and his choice alone, Jozef Venglos.

As far as possible I tried to prepare Jozef for what was likely to happen. He couldn't have been better about it. I had explained to him the whole history of Wim Jansen, Murdo MacLeod, David Hay *et al*. I had also told him about Egil Olsen and Mr Z and it seemed to me extremely important to try to eliminate as many surprises as possible, particularly as far as the coverage was concerned.

That Friday afternoon I also conducted a press conference with the Sunday newspapermen. In the course of that discussion I did make the point that we in Scotland tend to be very insular about our football and for that reason the reaction to the arrival of a world-renowned figure like Jozef Venglos was more difficult to appreciate. I referred to 'we in Scotland', which certainly includes me and I most certainly did not refer to Celtic supporters in particular. Nevertheless, that resulted in one Sunday newspaper carrying the banner headline 'Ignorant', indicating that I had accused Celtic supporters of such a characteristic. It really was about as low as you could get. No other Sunday newspaper took this line, just the *Sunday Mail*. Had I said anything like that you can be sure that they would all have picked up on it and made an issue of such an accusation.

What happened next was equally damaging. Daily newspapers picked up on that particular story and went to the Celtic Supporters' Association for a reaction. I sympathise with them. They cannot really be expected to appreciate fully how some tabloid newspapers operate. However, instead of saying 'I have no knowledge of Brown calling us ignorant and therefore will not comment', they immediately pursued their own line to defend Celtic supporters, quite naturally. The effect of such a defence is to attack me and, all in all, provides wonderful media fodder. However, it is a frightening departure from old journalistic principles, and it really is important for those in the sporting public eye not to rise to the bait of 'he said you are a plonker, what do you say about him?' syndrome.

Many people have asked me why so much popular journalism has gone this way and I think the answer is complicated. The main priority of newspapers is to increase circulation and there is a constant war in this respect among the various publications. This craving for new readers has led newspapers to increase the space available for sport since it has become widely acknowledged that lively sports coverage sells newspapers. In these cost-conscious days, however, newspapers are obviously reluctant to increase overheads, so the same journalists are now frequently being asked to provide many more column inches. The pressure is on and the result, I suppose inevitably, is a drop in standards.

There are similar difficulties with the broadcasting media. Since the cost of acquiring rights to football coverage has increased in recent times to realistic levels, the budgets of the radio and television companies have been stretched to the full. The result is massive cost-saving in all other areas to compensate for the additional money required to broadcast the football itself. The cheapest form of ancillary broadcasting is to pack studios with pundits and have them talk endlessly. That creates a tendency for those pundits who are given the opportunity of broadcasting to be as outspoken and outrageous as possible in order to capture an audience and retain their jobs.

It appears to me as though everyone in the football broadcasting world is seeking to emulate the late James Sanderson, who carved a niche for himself on Radio Clyde in the early 1980s by being aggressive, opinionated and frequently outrageously outspoken. In my opinion, no one has come close to matching Sanderson, and it strikes me that it was his wonderful capacity not to take himself seriously which distinguished him from all the pretenders. He knew exactly what he was doing and why he was doing it. He was wonderful, engaging company and never lost his sense of humour. Oh, I know he could be dangerous and caused his fellow journalists lots of grief by taking fliers on stories which were more in his imagination than in reality. This meant that editors of other newspapers were putting their reporters under enormous pressure to find out what Sanderson was talking about. But I do not recall him being maliciously vicious towards individuals in the game or perpetuating offensive myths about them. He is sadly missed.

I should declare an interest, of course, in that I did legal work for him. However, that puts him in precisely the same position as a host of the journalists currently on the scene, a fair percentage of whom attacked me viciously during my time at Celtic. Remember, I also did legal work for Murdo MacLeod and David Hay!

On that point, I found it interesting to note Murdo's explanation for the fact that although I had acted for him in the past our relationship had deteriorated. Like Hugh Keevins, his view was that I had changed, a view not shared by many of those who know me infinitely better.

The 'Ignorant' headline, as you can imagine, did me no favours. The Celtic-supporting *Sunday Mail* readers reacted badly and I was back in the area of threats. Sadly, many people buy only one Sunday newspaper. If it had been the *Sunday Mail* that weekend, readers would have been tempted to think the headline was true. If they had read other Sunday newspapers that day, they must have wondered why no one else had picked up on that headline from the same press conference.

The negative reporting on Saturday, 18 July, following my demolition in the tabloids the previous day gave rise to a reaction from Celtic supporters at Rugby Park on the Saturday afternoon. 'Stand up if you hate Jock Brown' emerged from the stand occupied by Celtic supporters. I was sitting in the directors' box beside Jozef Venglos, who was watching the Celtic players for the first time. The matter was not discussed between us but he certainly seemed to be bemused. For my own part, if there had been any lingering doubts about the power of the press, they had now been totally dispelled.

Interestingly enough, at 2.45 p.m. that afternoon I was standing in the tunnel with Jozef and Eric Black when my mobile telephone rang and the caller was Gerard Houllier. He wanted to speak to all three of us to wish us well for the season ahead. Naturally, we all reciprocated and I hope that Gerard turns out to be a huge success at Anfield.

In the opening twenty minutes of that match I wriggled uncomfortably in my seat beside Jozef. I had been extolling the virtues of our players, but at that stage in the match they frankly had not kicked a ball. Then Kilmarnock scored and suddenly we came to life. By halftime I was more relaxed and by the end of the match Jozef was expressing himself as very encouraged by what he had seen. The match had been won 2–1. Sadly, however, Morten Wieghorst had suffered a serious knee injury.

But the journey into season 1998–99 had begun. The European Champions' League was around the corner in the form of a qualifying tie against St Patrick's Athletic of Dublin. I was also able to remind Jozef of the signing deadline in the middle of August in respect of players who would be eligible to play in the Champions' League should we qualify, and that was a major priority.

Jozef's approach to team-building was, and is, meticulous. He indicated that it was imperative for him to have the opportunity to assess very carefully the existing squad of players before he decided what reinforcements might be required. Although I knew that the position he was adopting was absolutely right, from a personal point of view it created some frustration as I knew I would be the target of media abuse if there were to be any delays in bringing in new players.

But at the same time I knew that Jozef was correct. There was absolutely no point in bringing players to Celtic who were neither better than those already there nor offering a new dimension to the playing squad.

The other factor which concerned Jozef immensely from the first time I spoke to him about coming to Celtic was the fact that ten Celtic players were involved in the World Cup and Henrik Larsson was involved in international matches for Sweden right up until the beginning of June. He assured me that there would be inevitable fall-out from that in that the players would not have a proper break before the start of the new competitive season. The mental and emotional impact on them from playing at the highest level in the World Cup would also be such that there was sure to be a reaction when the new season got under way. He also indicated that the chances of injury were massively increased for those who had been involved in the World Cup because of the lack of rehabilitation time before the start of the season.

Jozef's knowledge and understanding of both sports science and the physiology of playing football is remarkable. I can recall Brian Scott, who is top class in his world of physiotherapy, expressing his disbelief at and admiration for Jozef's grasp of matters which were not normally in the domain of football coaches.

The other matter to be sorted out urgently was the question of the head coach's number two. Jozef had indicated a preference for a Scotsman and I had explained to him the role adopted by Eric Black for pre-season training and for the tour to Holland. He had met Eric at European coaching conventions and was fully aware of his playing background. He indicated to me that he would be happy to work with Eric from the outset to establish whether the necessary rapport existed for Eric to be appointed as his permanent number two.

The chemistry between them was instantly obvious. After a couple of training sessions and discussions with Eric, Jozef said he was perfectly satisfied that Eric was the right man and should be appointed. I resisted initially, saying that I was anxious that he should take more time over such an important appointment, bearing in mind the impact it would have on our development system at the club. I had explained to him the situation the previous season in which Wim Jansen and Murdo MacLeod had appeared to want nothing whatsoever to do with the youth development system. Since that was a very important element in Celtic's future, I had to be particularly careful to maintain continuity and not to create disruption. Accordingly, with Eric being so important to the continuity of the development system,

I was concerned about him being adopted as the permanent number two.

Jozef's answer was that Eric should continue as head of development and also operate as number two. 'The big difference you will find,' he told me, 'is that I will also be actively involved in the development side of the club and will help Eric as much as I possibly can. We will share the load since I think it is extremely important that the head coach is involved with the young players and with the young coaches.'

Nevertheless, he was persuaded to delay the final decision for a little longer to make sure that his initial impressions remained the same and that he was happy with Eric in that role.

One week after Jozef arrived at Celtic we were due to travel to Preston with the Under-21 team and the Under-18 team. It meant an 8 a.m. Sunday morning departure to watch the first match kicking off at 1 p.m. before moving on to our match at Deepdale, kicking off at 3 p.m. Jozef was on the trip only a matter of hours after a pre-season friendly match against Tottenham Hotspur at Celtic Park the previous day.

The impact he made on the young players and the coaching staff simply by his presence and his words of encouragement was immense. He addressed all the players on the team coach as we set off for home, delayed by a couple of hours because of a serious injury to John Convery, who needed hospital treatment for a damaged knee. On the trip north I was fascinated to see the development coaches in a cluster around Jozef discussing the two matches and obtaining his general views on the manner in which the matches had been played. The mood of isolation and, to some extent, despair felt by the coaching staff during the previous season was dispelled in a day.

The 0–0 home draw the following midweek against St Patrick's was a cause for some concern with a tricky second leg ahead, and around that time the vexed and universal issue of bonuses emerged.

CHAPTER 17

Working with Fergus

A satisfactory performance in the friendly against Tottenham Hotspur at Celtic Park on 25 July had the effect of calming nerves to some extent for the tricky midweek trip to Dublin for the European Cup qualifier. Any remaining tension was eliminated by an excellent goal from Harald Brattbakk after only eleven minutes and we were never in serious danger, although the second goal after the interval from Henrik Larsson was certainly welcome. I was subjected to more personal abuse from supporters over there. The great difficulty was that certain elements of the press had seen fit to report the Kilmarnock chants in some detail, and with some exaggeration, so that something of a trend had been set.

But the question of personal abuse took on a new dimension on Saturday, 1 August. It was the day Celtic supporters had been waiting ten years for. The unfurling of the league championship flag was scheduled to take place just before the opening league match of the season against Dunfermline Athletic. The tragedy was that the negativity perpetuated by certain popular elements of the media resulted in a reaction from Celtic supporters which reflected absolutely no credit upon them and sullied the great name of Celtic Football Club. Fergus McCann, the man who had written personal cheques for millions of pounds to save the club and who had presided over the most amazing miracle, I would suggest in the history of Scottish football, was roundly booed by a significant section of the crowd. It defied belief.

Although Fergus had already demonstrated the skin of a rhinoceros during his time rescuing and rebuilding the club, he was undoubtedly shaken by this reaction on what should have been a day of triumph. His wife, Elspeth, who was only a very occasional attender at matches, was present to experience this shameful incident in the history of Celtic. My heart went out to both of them. Even a number of the players, including some who were not natural soulmates of the chairman, were appalled and shocked by the reaction.

I could not see past this episode when it came to write my weekly column in the *Celtic View*. I expressed the opinion that in the year 2050, when people were considering the history of Celtic, two names would be acknowledged as having had the greatest impact on the club's fortunes. These men were Jock Stein and Fergus McCann. In these circumstances, I could not begin to understand why there should be such an appalling reaction at the unfurling of the championship flag.

That issue of the *Celtic View* was scarcely on the streets when I was being pilloried for comparing Fergus McCann with Jock Stein. I cannot recall many tabloid reports of what I had said in the *Celtic View* which acknowledged my very important reference to the year 2050. The whole point of that was to show that while Fergus McCann may not have received the credit to which he was entitled during his tenure at Celtic Park, history would show the incredible impact he made. By 2050 there would be few who could recall personal issues, the assassination of character, and whether Fergus was tall, short, thin or fat. They would simply assess objectively and dispassionately within the terms of the history of the club the fact that it was effectively out of business in March 1994 yet within four and a half years had occupied the finest club stadium in the United Kingdom and unfurled the league championship flag. For the first time, I used the expression that if I had rescued a toddler from a burning building, certain elements of the press would portray me as a child molester.

My regular column with the *Celtic View* ended. The official reason was that the recently appointed editor, Joe Sullivan, a good man, had decided that a regular weekly column was unfair in that there would be weeks when I had nothing really to say and space was at a premium in that successful publication. He indicated that he preferred to use material from me only when circumstances justified this. I agreed with this line of thinking and co-operated fully, although I now believe I was wrong. However, that was the official line presented in kindly fashion to me. I suspect that more powerful forces had decided there was little point in me providing further cannon fodder for certain tabloid newspapers by writing anything at all in the club newspaper.

The following Saturday saw the official opening of the Jock Stein Stand to complete the stadium, with Mrs Jean Stein as guest of honour. I said quietly to Fergus during that week that if I were in his shoes I would be sorely tempted to complete the opening of the stand and then announce my immediate departure for sunny and more appreciative climes. Such an early departure was never in his contemplation. To the immense credit of the vast majority of excellent Celtic supporters, Fergus's reception on 8 August was a good one, demonstrating what was felt by so many people in relation to the previous week's disgrace.

The question I was asked most frequently after arriving at Celtic in June 1997 was: 'What is it like working with Fergus?' The implication behind the question always seemed to be that it was expected that working with him would be, to say the least, difficult, if not impossible. In fact, the question was sometimes adjusted into more of a statement: 'It must be very tough working with Fergus?'

Yes, it was certainly challenging. But for me it was never a problem. He is razor-sharp mentally, totally focused, utterly determined and would not know how to begin to ingratiate himself with anyone. He calls a spade a spade and can be immensely impatient and frequently intolerant. He certainly doesn't suffer fools gladly, nor is he too adept at trying to spare people's feelings when he has a point to make.

However, for such a single-minded operator he has one outstanding quality. He will listen to an alternative point of view and is capable of being persuaded that his original position should be adjusted. He certainly respects people who will argue with him and debate issues. Sometimes you win, sometimes you lose, but I was never conscious of any grudge being held or any adverse reaction being taken to someone who made a forceful point in good faith. You can always work with someone like that. What you could never do with Fergus was tell him that a problem had emerged without being prepared to offer a recommended solution. Every opportunity would be given to justify the recommendation and after a healthy debate a decision would be reached.

Probably the most difficult aspect of working with Fergus for me was finding myself constantly in the buffer zone between him and the board on one side and the coaches and players on the other. I certainly saw it as a major element in my job to try to bridge any gap between the two sides as effectively as possible. However, my position was frequently extremely difficult, especially when Wim Jansen was head coach.

The old – and, dare I say it, obsolescent – football culture is something which Fergus was determined to change. He is absolutely right in that many elements of that culture do require changing in the modern era. The question is whether this should be done by the bludgeon or the rapier. Neither Fergus nor I was ever afraid of confrontation, but I think I was naturally more able to introduce compromise and diplomacy. That in itself sometimes caused confrontation! But you knew where you stood with him. You could be very confident that he would not be saying something behind your back that he was not prepared to say to your face. He does not want to be surrounded by puppets or 'yes men', and while in the last analysis you knew that the majority shareholder, chairman, managing director and chief executive, all of which he was, would have his way in terms of the final decision, you were never too inhibited to state a case which conflicted with his view. It was also perfectly acceptable to state such a case forcibly.

There was one occasion on which there was an issue which required careful deliberation. After substantial debate, I received an instruction to take a course of action with which I did not agree. However, it was an instruction and Fergus expected instructions to be obeyed. The matter troubled me greatly. As a result, I spent a night putting my thoughts on paper and handed Fergus a lengthy handwritten note the following morning. It set out my arguments in detail and finished with a request that his instruction be withdrawn or amended. We met at lunchtime and I was not at all sure what to expect. Not for the first time, he surprised me. He said that I had clearly given substantial thought to the matter in hand and it was obviously something which I felt strongly about. He acknowledged the merits in the points made and withdrew the instruction.

Another time he surprised me was soon after I had joined the club when there were lots of issues to contend with and intense media scrutiny of every move. He came into my room in the middle of the day and asked what my plans were for lunch. I replied that I had not given the matter much thought and was too intent on tackling the multiplicity of issues requiring attention.

'Come on,' he said, 'let's go somewhere for lunch.'

We then left the stadium and went to a small restaurant on the outskirts of the city where we had an excellent lunch discussing everything except Celtic. He was in sparkling form and excellent company. He couldn't have been more removed from the image regularly presented within the media. He had clearly formed the view that it was time for us both to breathe.

So the answer to the basic question about working with Fergus is that it was challenging, enlightening and only occasionally exasperating, when I couldn't get him to see things my way. He expected, and gave, total honesty and directness and he never, ever lost sight of his vision for Celtic. He enriched my professional career in terms of experience.

I was constantly pressing Jozef Venglos to identify any weakness in the team, and potential recruits to strengthen the squad, prior to the European deadline in the middle of August. Jozef would not be rushed. He would not make a signing for the sake of it. He kept insisting that any player brought in must either be better than players already in the squad or add a new dimension to the squad's play. Eventually he did identify three players he wished to pursue. Each one matched the criteria of improving the squad or adding a new dimension. In each case the players' clubs would not sell.

It is nonsense to suggest that every player has his price. At that stage in the season, players of genuine quality were badly wanted by their existing clubs and it was certainly not a time when they wished to sell. I made the observation at one supporters' meeting that if anyone approached me to purchase Henrik Larsson, what response did they want me to give? I explained that I would not accept a bid at any price for Larsson and everyone acknowledged that I was correct. I then made the point that other clubs had their Henrik Larssons and it was that quality of player we were trying to buy. It was no wonder that in these circumstances the selling clubs would not agree to a deal.

A fourth player was actively pursued before the European deadline, with the same result. He was not for sale at any price. Accordingly, the deadline came and went without new recruits and that gave the media a field day, with yours truly taking the brunt of the abuse. What I could not understand was the fact that anyone actually believed that I was reluctant to complete any purchases. No one had a greater incentive than I to complete deals. However, if it ever reaches the stage where you sign a three-legged Martian with a big name for £5 million simply to take the pressure off yourself, it is certainly time to quit.

That's another mystery as far as I am concerned. Generally speaking, there appears to be a view abroad that the only signing worth having is one which costs a fortune. Nowadays, that simply does not make sense. Many players have contractual terms which make it possible for their contracts to be purchased at a relatively modest fee. The Bosman ruling has also had a marked effect on transfer fees, although it has had a similar upward-spiralling effect on players' wages. There appeared to be no real excitement when Henrik Larsson was signed from Feyenoord at a fee of £650,000. Had the price been £6 million then he would probably have received a tumultuous welcome. The tragedy is that you can spend £6 million without any guarantee of the player being a huge success and you can spend £650,000 and have an out-and-out bargain.

Instead of being praised for the prudent acquisition of outstanding players, there is a mentality abroad which prefers to take up the popular media theme of the club being penny-pinching and mean. Surely the whole idea is to conduct your business sensibly, prudently and to the best possible long-term effect on the club? It is not difficult to think of examples of clubs who have lived to regret spending millions of pounds on players who have flopped. I can recall being offered a player signed for millions at less than half his purchase price well inside one year – and he was still of no interest to the head coach!

Apply that to the incredible Glasgow situation. I have often wondered what kind of press reaction there would have been if Celtic had spent £4 million on Sebastian Rozenthal, a similar amount on Lorenzo Amoruso and £3 million on Daniel Prodan, without obtaining the benefit of the services of two of them until now and the services of Amoruso only after one year's absence. Celtic would have been slaughtered.

Yet the clamour for new signings never ended, and the more expensive, the better. Jozef Venglos's highly responsible view was that while it might be possible to bring in players of similar quality to those at Celtic when he arrived, it was not going to be easy to bring in better ones, especially in the early part of a season when most clubs were anxious to hold on to their best players. It really demonstrates the need for pre-planning starting in the early months of the year so that you are in the market place at the appropriate time towards the end of a season and into the close season.

It was on that basis that I resented accusations levelled at me attributing blame for not bringing in new players for the European campaign when culpability lay fairly and squarely on the shoulders of the former head coach, who had stopped carrying out a vital part of his duties some three months before he left.

It was similarly unfair to direct any criticism towards Jozef Venglos whose overriding interest from the moment he arrived at Celtic was what was best for the club, not for him as an individual. That, for me, is the mark of the true professional. Jozef Venglos knew perfectly well that he could curry favour with Celtic supporters by splashing out money on virtually anyone, but he refused to do that until he was absolutely certain that the criteria he thought were right for Celtic were met.

Talking of press reaction takes us to Pittodrie on 16 August, a Sunday evening televised match in the league. Having outplayed Aberdeen for large sections of the match, we contrived to miss two penalty kicks and find ourselves three down in the most bizarre fashion. In the middle of the second half, with the score still 3–0 to Aberdeen, one of the directors leaned across to me and said, 'Do you realise that you will be blamed in tomorrow's press for missing these penalties?' The only possible reaction was to laugh. At that point the Sky Television cameras caught me and that was enough for one of the tabloids to take a photograph from the TV screen and ridicule me for laughing when the team was three goals down.

In the closing stages of the match we pulled a goal back, converted another penalty, and had the most stonewall of them all turned down to lose in the end by the odd goal. That result came after the stadium-opening match against Liverpool the previous week, when cordial relations with Gerard Houllier were reinforced.

By the time of the Aberdeen match, my treatment from many sections of the media was viciously unrestrained and certainly not in the interests of the club. I had been blamed for the delay in bringing in the head coach and then for the delay in bringing in new players. Comparisons with the lavish spending of Rangers were constantly made, although there were very few references to the fact that seventeen players who had played first-team football for Rangers had left the club over the summer whereas every one of the twenty-two-man Celtic first-team squad which had delivered the championship was still at Celtic and youngsters like Mark Burchill and John Paul McBride were pushing for recognition. The nine players who had arrived over the previous year had no doubt settled even better for the season about to start, but the message constantly being hammered home by supporters, fuelled by the media, was 'Spend the money'.

There were accusations directed towards Fergus McCann at that time that he had cheated the supporters by not spending their season-ticket money on new players. I am always intrigued by the willingness of people to spend other people's money, usually with the same pound requiring to be spent in several different directions. Explaining the fact that season-ticket money from 52,000 supporters did not pay the club's wage bill cut no ice. People seemed to want the same season-ticket money to be used to complete the building of the stadium, for the purchase of new players, for paying the steadily spiralling salaries to players, and for building a state-of-the-art training complex, quite apart from meeting the bills generated by normal business running costs. Depending upon your perspective, the tendency is to focus on the element which you believe to be most important and seek to have money generated diverted in that direction. The trouble is that there were five competing claims, reduced now to four by the completion of the stadium.

Having said that, there was never any restriction whatsoever imposed by the board on the recruitment of new players either in season 1997–98 or 1998–99. Indeed, with the unrelenting pressure from all sources to buy players, the directors were as anxious as anyone else to complete deals, subject to retaining a sense of perspective to ensure that any deals were sensible ones. But no one wanted to bring in players more than I did, followed very closely indeed by Jozef Venglos and Eric Black. The difficulty was finding the right ones.

One of these emerged from our second qualifying tie in the European Champions' League against Croatia Zagreb. Both Kenny McDowall and Jozef Venglos had travelled to watch the Croatian side play in separate matches and both had identified Mark Viduka as the ideal type of striker to add to the Celtic squad. In the first leg at Celtic Park, when we did extremely well to win the match by one goal to nil and just missed out on a second before the end, Viduka impressed not only the coaching staff but also the Celtic players and, in particular, centre-backs Marc Rieper and Alan Stubbs.

Jozef indicated to me after that match that once the second leg was over he would like to bring Viduka to Celtic. Obviously that would be easier if we managed to overcome the Croatians, but even if we did not, we should be determined to try to bring the big striker to the club.

Sadly, things did not go well for us in Zagreb in the second leg and we lost by three goals to nil with a depleted side. Immediately afterwards, I began negotiations for Viduka.

CHAPTER 18

Bonuses!

At that early stage of the season we were also treated to what I considered to be the unedifying spectacle of Wim Jansen and Murdo MacLeod creating a media circus by attending matches at Celtic Park. There is an unwritten protocol among football people that once you have left a club, regardless of the circumstances, you stay away for a reasonable length of time and await an invitation to return. Devoted Celtic men like Tommy Burns have acknowledged that by their absence, despite the fact that Tommy would most certainly have been a thoroughly welcome visitor at Celtic Park during my time. The governing rule as far as I am concerned is to consider what is in the best interests of the club.

The arrival of Wim Jansen and Murdo MacLeod at our opening league match on 1 August could scarcely have been deemed to have been in the interests of the club, since it attracted huge media interest in the day or two before the match and deflected from the real business of getting off to a good start. Once again it provided an opportunity for sections of the media to direct negativity towards the club at a crucial time. It also failed, in my opinion, to show adequate respect for the new head coach by staying away. My own reaction was simply to stay away from them and ensure that I was not dragged into any kind of media reaction. Contrary to some reports, there was no question whatsoever of either of them being asked to leave.

Since my own departure I have had invitations – indeed, I have a standing invitation – to attend matches at Celtic Park whenever I wish. I would love to go because I hate missing any match but, adhering to the principle of what is best for the club, it seems obvious to me I should not permit any distraction from the real business of the club by generating media interest in my attendance.

There was always an overriding press interest in respect of Wim Jansen and Murdo MacLeod. I feared other people were using them to advance their own agendas, and while I am not at all convinced that Wim would have grasped the possibility of being used, I am sure Murdo was well versed and astute enough to have known exactly what he was doing. But the number of people in the game who expressed their outrage and disbelief at Wim and Murdo attending matches as they did was substantial. It certainly did Murdo, in particular, no good whatsoever in the eyes of the Scottish footballing world.

Around this time I also had a lengthy discussion with Paul Lambert, who appeared to have been extremely vocal during the World Cup about all matters concerning Celtic. He apparently constantly made veiled references to being unhappy about his perception of his status at the club as far as I was concerned. He had never expressed this directly to me before, but he came to see me on his return to the club after the World Cup since he had clearly become wound up and agitated about the notion that I had delayed his transfer to Celtic and did not rate him as a player.

His attitude appeared to have been exacerbated by the nonsense written by Murdo MacLeod in his Sunday tabloid articles in which he perpetuated that myth. Accordingly, I welcomed the opportunity to have an open discussion with Paul with a view to clearing the air and resolving matters. I actually spent the best part of a couple of hours with him discussing the matter in detail. I explained to him what had happened in the conversation between David Hay and Jim Melrose and also about the difficulties in persuading Borussia Dortmund to let him go.

While I was perfectly happy to discuss this with him, I tried to reassure him that I did, in fact, rate him as a player and that under no circumstances was I party to any delay in his arrival. On the contrary, I had been determined to bring him to the club at the earliest opportunity and as far as I am concerned I did so. I could not understand why it seemed to be so important to him.

He kept saying to me, 'If you think I am not a good player, simply tell me that and I will accept it and we shall get on with our lives.' I told him that if that had been the case I would be quite happy to tell him so privately, but it was not the truth and I was not prepared to lie to him. At the same time, I kept asking him to explain why it mattered to him so much, since the only opinion which mattered was that of the head coach, and in both Wim Jansen and Jozef Venglos he had admirers who wanted him in the team. But he made reference to the fact that his family had been upset by the delay in him arriving at Celtic. He had been told that I was the reason for that. I did try to explain to him that he was listening to people with agendas in circumstances where I had nothing to gain. He made the remarkable observation that while he noted what I was saying, it was in conflict with what he had been told by six other people. Among the six I would expect Wim Jansen, Murdo MacLeod, David Hay, Jim Melrose and probably his new agent Gordon Smith. I had never passed any opinion on his ability to any of them, except of a positive nature.

Paul remained unconvinced. I finished up by telling him that he had heard what I had to say and should not work on the basis that if one person says something to the contrary and repeats that to five other people, that results in six witnesses. In any event, he was at the club, I was delighted he was at the club, and I had no part to play in his selection for matches or any other aspect of his work until the time came to discuss a new contract.

Paul also made an issue of the fact that I had insisted on setting up media training facilities for the players to assist them in their dealings with the press and radio and television. That is a matter which ought to have remained private but which he saw fit to mention publicly. He was adamant that he would have no part of any such training since he was a senior professional and did not need it. He simply gave further strength to my argument that those who protest most loudly against something like that are usually those who need it most. That certainly applies to Paul, in my opinion.

He finished up expressing his appreciation for the time given to him to discuss the matter and said that he would go and consider carefully all that had been said at the meeting. For my part, I welcomed the opportunity to have the matter aired and left it entirely up to him to decide who to believe. Only when his book was published did I find out his decision! It was a pity that he could not be privy to the minutes of board meetings over the relevant period discussing the efforts made to overcome the hurdles to bring him to Celtic.

Another factor among the many which guaranteed that there could never be any question of boredom at Celtic Park related to bonuses. I'm sure there isn't a club in the country which does not have differences of opinion internally about the question of bonuses but in Celtic's case that tends to be defined as 'turmoil'.

My first involvement with bonuses was fairly early in my time at Celtic, when I had been examining all the contracts and reached the conclusion that the bonus system which had been in place for some considerable time was out of date and required revamping. To that end I had a number of discussions with the players' representatives,

Tommy Boyd and Gordon Marshall, with a view to coming up with a satisfactory, modernised scheme. One of the principles of a bonus system which I think is essential in modern times is that all players are treated the same as far as bonuses are concerned, despite the fact that their wages can differ significantly. The players also appeared to accept that view, so what we were looking for was an overall scheme affecting all the players which was fair in all circumstances and workable in the interests of all parties.

After several meetings with Tommy and Gordon I was able to obtain from the directors an alternative bonus plan to be offered to the players in place of the existing plan. Since this was mid-season, the proposal was that the players could either remain with the existing bonus plan or switch to the newly proposed plan which carried greater potential benefits, but involved greater risks. The players opted to continue with the old system for the rest of season 1997–98 on the basis that fresh discussions would take place to come into effect for the 1998–99 season. On that basis, all bonus discussions were put on the back-burner while the serious business of winning the championship was in process.

During the close season, after further consultation with the directors, I put to Tommy Boyd on behalf of the players a proposed new bonus system to take into account the European Champions' League and all the domestic competitions. As is normal in the world of football, the element which attracted the attention was the first one likely to come into force, namely the European Champions' League bonuses. Quite simply, the players did not believe they were being rewarded adequately for success in Europe, and Tom made that point to me.

Indeed, prior to the second-leg match against St Patrick's Athletic in Dublin I had a very open and frank discussion with all the players on the subject of bonuses. At that point, one element which disturbed them was the fact that the club had offered a bonus on qualification for the Champions' League, which meant beating both St Patrick's and Croatia Zagreb. The players believed that there should be a separate bonus for beating St Patrick's, regardless of whether or not they were successful against Croatia Zagreb.

There were obviously two arguments. What really mattered to the club was qualification for the Champions' League and they were prepared to pay handsomely in terms of bonuses for that kind of success. Losing to St Patrick's, with all due respect to the Irish club, should not have been contemplated and victory was scarcely worthy of a separate bonus. However, in order to qualify for the UEFA Cup, at least, it was essential for the club to overcome St Patrick's. Failure to beat the Dublin side would mean not only being out of the Champions' League but also being out of the UEFA Cup. Success against St Patrick's and failure against Croatia Zagreb would mean a place in the UEFA Cup and accordingly further revenue for the club.

At the request of Tom Boyd I met with all nineteen players in the team hotel in Dublin the evening before the St Pat's match. Now I've appeared in courts all over the land and made speeches before hundreds of people at home and abroad, but I can assure you there is nothing more daunting than facing, single-handedly, a squad of top-class professional players who have a grievance!

Having debated the bonus issue for the best part of an hour, I took on board the normal footballer's mentality of expecting a bonus for success in virtually any match and, in particular, the fact that success against St Patrick's guaranteed extra revenue for the club by means of the UEFA Cup at least. Accordingly, I managed to persuade Fergus on the day of the match that there was merit in offering a separate bonus, and that indeed is what happened.

There were a couple of significant factors from these discussions. First, Fergus McCann was not the kind of dictator he was regularly made out to be, and second, the club was prepared to enter into dialogue and listen to cogent arguments made on such matters. This was hardly in keeping with the image popularly portrayed.

Tom Boyd's handling of the issue was also very significant. I advised him of Fergus's decision just before the pre-match meal, at around 4.30 p.m. He did not tell the players until after the match had been won. Why not?

'I decided I did not want to deflect the players from their concentration on the job in hand,' he told me. 'I also wanted to make a point about the character of the players. They will give their all, regardless.'

It was an approach which was intelligent, perceptive and highly responsible.

That matter having been resolved, in my opinion responsibly and satisfactorily, the big public issue arose around the Croatia Zagreb match. It is now a matter of public record that the bonus offered to the squad for beating Croatia Zagreb and qualifying for the Champions' League was £280,000. The distribution of that sum of money was to be entirely at the discretion of the players. If they wanted to divide the money amongst only those who took the field of play, the club would co-operate, whereas if they preferred to distribute the bonus funds evenly among the first-team squad, including injured players, then that would also be acceptable.

That accounts for the varying stories appearing in the press about how much each man would receive. If fourteen players were to share the bonus then it would be £20,000 per man, whereas if the entire first-team squad was to share evenly then you had to divide the total sum by twenty-two or however many made up the first-team training squad. That would reduce the individual payments. The players believed that sum was not enough. They were not persuaded by the fact that it was by far the largest bonus ever offered to a Celtic team. Their view was that the implications of qualifying for the Champions' League in terms of revenue to the club were so vast that they should receive greater rewards. The view of the directors was that the sum offered was more than fair.

It all became a public issue a couple of days before the first-leg match against Croatia Zagreb when three of the players were scheduled to take part in a photo shoot for the club sponsors, Umbro. The three involved were Marc Rieper, Jackie McNamara and Regi Blinker. That morning, before training, the players had told me that they did not believe the bonus was satisfactory and I had made it clear that there would be no movement. I was asked if only Fergus McCann could authorise improvement on the bonus and I confirmed that that was the case. They then asked if they could make a case directly to Fergus. I undertook to ask him if he was prepared to meet them.

While the players were at training I duly discussed the matter with Fergus and he indicated that he would be prepared to talk to the players the following day. I reported this back to Tom Boyd after the players returned from training. However, the players, in their wisdom, decided to make a gesture to demonstrate the strength of their feelings on the bonus issue by boycotting the Umbro photo shoot which was scheduled for 1 p.m. that Monday. I should make it clear that this was not a decision reached only by the three participants but by the entire playing squad. I felt immensely sorry for the three individuals concerned in that they were singled out for adverse treatment by some elements of the media when they were simply doing what had been agreed by the whole squad.

When this news was conveyed to me around 1 p.m. by Tom Boyd, I immediately recognised the implications. I explained to Tom what they would be. Celtic would lead the radio and television news bulletins and would be all over the newspapers the following morning in negative circumstances. The players would be accused of being greedy and there was no way in which there could be winners from such a course of action. While Tom demonstrated solidarity with his team-mates, I detected that he realised, if only then, what was about to happen. I asked him if I could see all the players and try to persuade them directly, or at least see the three players who had been withdrawn. He disappeared to the dressing-room and returned to say that most of the players had gone and there would be no possibility of the overall position changing without the consent of every player.

As we were discussing the matter, the media room upstairs was full of journalists and photographers. The officials from Umbro were present and accordingly there was no way in the world the issue would not become public. Fergus was brought into the picture, and to say that he was less than happy is an understatement. He decided that he would meet with the press and explain to them directly that the reason for the absence of the players from the scheduled photo shoot related to their dissatisfaction with the bonus on offer for the Croatia Zagreb game, notwithstanding the fact that he had agreed to meet them the following day to discuss matters further.

The news exploded, just as we all knew it would, with the effect that the meeting scheduled for the following morning was sure to be difficult. The meeting duly took place in an extremely tense atmosphere. Fergus told the players that the bonus of £280,000 was being reduced by £50,000, which was going to be donated to charity, leaving £230,000 available for winning the match. There was no question of that figure being adjusted. The entire meeting lasted no longer than ten minutes. That information was then conveyed to the media, who had already been speculating on the amount being offered to the players.

In the normal fashion, the squad departed for a hotel on the Tuesday evening before the match on the Wednesday night and that evening a statement was issued from the team hotel on behalf of the players to the effect that they were prepared to sacrifice the entire bonus to charity if Fergus, on behalf of the club, would commit the appropriate sum, win or lose. As the players should have known, Fergus called their bluff.

The obvious concern was how this whole unsavoury matter would affect the team's performance on the Wednesday night at Celtic Park. The players, to their immense credit, showed no evidence whatsoever of any reaction and they played extremely well to win the match by one goal to nil. However, the weight of public opinion was solidly behind the club and against the players. It was obviously very difficult for thousands of supporters to accept that players were unhappy with a bonus, on top of their wages, which was more than many of them earn in a year.

The mistake made by the players was allowing the matter to become public by failing to attend the photo shoot. What upset me was the fact that this decision appeared to have been taken on an *ad hoc* basis after training and without full and proper consideration. Had it been suggested to me at my meeting that morning that there was a possibility of boycotting the photo shoot, I would have gone to any lengths necessary to persuade the players this was a huge mistake. I have no doubt that many of them, if not all, acknowledge now that what they saw as a gesture of strength of feeling and solidarity was mistimed and misdirected.

It certainly did not help relations between the players and the club, or at least Fergus. For my own part, despite the manner in which I was pilloried in the press for botching the bonus discussions, my dealings with the players remained civilised and cordial. In particular, I could only compliment Tom Boyd on his professionalism in conducting our many discussions in a totally civilised fashion while never losing sight of his obligations to represent the players in the dressing-room. In my professional life I have been involved in hosts of such negotiations and I would rank Tom Boyd alongside many lawyers and experienced businessmen for the manner in which he represented his team-mates, remaining courteous yet extremely forceful without ever being aggressive or offensive. Gordon Marshall, incidentally, who left the club before matters boiled over, was similarly impressive. They are both fine men as well as excellent footballers, and the skills they would have needed to deal with the diverse opinions and attitudes in the dressing-room must have been substantial.

As I had feared, however, for some time afterwards there were no letters columns in newspapers, phone-ins on radio or television or any sporting debates which did not include the Celtic bonus issue. Strangely enough, within Celtic Park the issue was nothing like so prominent. Following further discussions I had with Tom Boyd it was agreed that the players would appoint an agent to represent them collectively on bonus matters and thus defuse the issue in terms of personality. In the meantime, it was agreed that the matter would not be discussed further either internally or publicly. The players had their final say by issuing a statement to which I, on behalf of the club, decided not to respond, and from that point it was agreed that it would be business as usual, with the appointed agent left to deal with the club on the question of bonuses.

The unfortunate side effect of the press coverage of the bonus issue was that the players decided to withdraw their co-operation from the media because of what they saw as totally unfair treatment. The trouble with that kind of decision is that in the fullness of time a decision must be taken to reverse it and difficulty was sure to arise within that process. The players also indicated their reluctance to become involved in club events of a public relations, promotions or sponsorship nature, although Tom Boyd was explicit in making it clear to me that there would be no question of charitable events being excluded from their activities. As it happened, normal relations in these matters were restored after a fairly short time, although the difficulties the players had with the press lasted longer.

They lasted longer, in fact, than the second leg in Zagreb two weeks later, when a *Daily Record* reporter left a message on the voice mail in Darren Jackson's hotel room to the effect that he wanted a return call because he understood that a member of Darren's family had committed suicide. That resulted in feverish telephone calls to Scotland to ascertain that the 'report' was total nonsense, but that was not established before Darren had endured substantial anguish.

My own position in this whole sorry situation was clear. I was utterly convinced that it was not in the interests of the club or the players for me to comment on bonuses or press bans. Under no circumstances was I prepared to condemn the players publicly for any of their actions, and while I might have been able to alleviate the pressure on myself by certain warblings to the media, I was convinced that this was a dereliction of my duties to the club and the players. As a result I kept silent publicly, although day-to-day dialogue with the players continued without strain and with the normal cordiality.

A few days after the Croatia Zagreb second leg I was back in Zagreb attempting to negotiate the deal to bring Mark Viduka to Celtic. While standing in the shower in my hotel room at 7.30 in the morning, I heard Sky News convey the news that the *Daily Record* was reporting that the brothers Brown, Craig, the Scotland manager, and Jock, the general manager of Celtic, were on borrowed time. I couldn't suppress a smile. It turned out to be material printed under a heading 'The Brothers Dim'.

I consoled myself with the thought that if I was as dim as Craig or as incompetent as he was, I would settle for that, bearing in mind the magnificent job he has done for Scotland.

CHAPTER 19

Zagreb and Beyond

I had gone to Zagreb on the understanding that the Croatians were prepared to discuss the transfer of Mark Viduka immediately, notwithstanding their success in reaching the Champions' League. In order to make the journey at the time in question I had to intimate an apology for non-attendance at the Supporters' Association delegates' meeting which was to take place on that particular Sunday afternoon.

During season 1997–98 I attended such meetings on a Sunday once a month to update supporters and answer questions. I believe I missed only one such meeting because of business over that entire season. On no occasion did Wim Jansen or Murdo MacLeod offer to attend despite the fact that the supporters would have been delighted to see them.

I used to be perfectly happy attending these meetings because it gave me the opportunity to answer a host of questions which frequently stemmed from tabloid coverage and often bore little relation to reality. At the same time, the distaste shown by the delegates towards certain of these tabloids was intense. But it did not stop them initially treating as accurate reports which were simply speculative or fictional.

Accordingly, I did not expect any great difficulty in intimating my apology for this particular meeting at the beginning of September because I was off on important club business. However, *en route* for Zagreb on the Saturday afternoon while Scotland were playing an international match leaving the club card clear, I received a telephone call from Peter McLean advising me that the supporters were extremely perturbed that I would not be at their meeting the following day. I was told that the whole meeting had been set aside for a question-and-answer session with me and it was a matter of immense importance that I attended to deal with all the queries. I had not been given such information before and immediately indicated to Peter that he should revert to the supporters' executive and tell them that I was prepared to accept by fax to my hotel as many questions as they wanted to give me on the understanding that I would give them written replies prior to their delegates' meeting the following day at 2 p.m. This offer was not taken up.

On the Sunday I received another call from Peter to tell me that a newspaper had contacted him asking him to confirm what he or I knew about a vote of no-confidence being taken in me following my absence from the delegates' meeting. It turned out that such a vote had taken place without me being given notice of the subject matter of the meeting or any opportunity to speak further, and despite the fact that my offer to provide answers to any number of questions by fax had not been taken up.

I realised then that the plethora of negative press comment, not to mention the vicious personal attacks, had clearly had a marked effect on the Supporters' Association, although in view of my previous cordial meetings with them I was very disappointed that they saw fit to proceed in such a clandestine fashion and make judgements without hearing my version of events. It appeared that the principal matter which caused them concern was the suggestion that I had lied to them in May about the situation relating to the head coach. I hadn't, but it appeared as though the executive had conveyed to the membership quite strongly that the appointment of the head coach was imminent on the basis of my honest disclosure to them at our meeting in May. I did not have the opportunity, of course, of explaining to the delegates face to face exactly what had happened in relation to Egil Olsen so that any allegations of lying could be withdrawn.

In the meantime, I arrived in Zagreb around 3.30 p.m. I was accompanied on the trip by two agents from London appointed by Croatia Zagreb. I understood that the club officials were aware of my journey and my arrival time. Accordingly, I was somewhat taken aback when it was suggested on arrival at Zagreb Airport that we should go for a coffee while one of the agents called the club to find out what was going on. That information was not readily available, because apparently there was a meeting in progress. There were always 'meetings' in progress in Zagreb, in my experience.

However, I sat in the airport for more than an hour before going by taxi to a hotel in the city centre. Further phone calls were made but 'meetings' were still in progress. Eventually, at around 7.30 p.m., I was told that the general manager of Croatia Zagreb would be calling to meet us in the hotel later. At around 9 p.m. a very bleary-eyed general manager appeared to report on the lengthy nature of his day, which had apparently commenced at 7.30 a.m., and to advise me that I should report to the club stadium the following day at 9.30 a.m. to discuss Mark Viduka. He was not prepared to discuss anything there and then but would be at the meeting the following morning. With that, he left. I was less than pleased at being left hanging around half the afternoon and the entire evening when Croatia Zagreb knew of my trip and its purpose.

At 9.30 a.m. I duly appeared at the Croatia Zagreb stadium with the two agents from London. Three of their officials came into the meeting to tell me that they had decided not to sell Mark Viduka until they were out of the European Champions' Cup. The fact that this was totally in conflict with the information I had received to prompt my journey was of no consequence or interest. I had booked a return flight for the following day on the basis that I hoped not only to agree terms with the club but also to begin discussions with Mark Viduka himself that day, but as the whole visit had turned out to be a complete waste of time I made my way straight to the airport to catch an earlier flight to London.

My involvement in the whole Viduka affair was fascinating. I can recall a total of ten agents who were involved in one way or another with the deal. That does not take into account the number of agents who contacted me claiming to be Viduka's agent when, in fact, they were only hoping to be. I received many calls from people telling me that they acted for Viduka and asking if we were interested in him and, if so, on what terms. Had I been foolish enough to accept as accurate the terms of such phone calls the agents concerned would no doubt have reverted to Viduka to tell him that he was the only agent who could do the deal with Celtic since he had made direct contact with me and had discussed terms.

I found that the only way to function in these circumstances was to indicate to any agent claiming to act for Viduka that he should forward to me by fax a copy of the mandate signed by Viduka authorising him to act. That usually ended the conversation. Viduka's real agents only became apparent about seven weeks after my initial visit to Zagreb.

Having returned home a day early I was able to report fully to Fergus and discuss not only the Viduka situation but also the attitude adopted by the Supporters' Association. In the course of that conversation I said to him, 'You realise that you will have to sacrifice me.' He asked what I meant. I explained that it was inevitable that I would have to leave the club as a sacrifice in view of the manner in which the media treatment had stirred up the supporters, and in view of the fact that there appeared to be no way in which certain elements of the media would be deflected from their clear intention of beating me into submission and forcing me to leave the club.

Fergus was totally supportive. He indicated that he would resist such action and when I replied that, while I appreciated his support, he had to realise that such an outcome was inevitable, he refused to accept this. I repeated that my leaving the club was inevitable. It need not happen immediately but it was only a matter of time. Fergus appeared genuinely surprised and perturbed at what I was saying but I do believe that it dawned on him that I was right.

The discussion about the need for me to be sacrificed in September came shortly before the club's AGM. As far as some sections of the media were concerned, this was an occasion on which I was to be strung up metaphorically by thousands of angry shareholders. But it didn't turn out that way. Oh, yes, there were a number of rabble-rousers, but in percentage terms they were small. If 2,000 people are sitting quietly when the platform party arrives on stage and 100 start booing and jeering, obviously the only ones you will hear will be those who are booing and jeering.

I found the whole experience utterly remarkable. In circumstances where a club was showing outstanding financial results, with two out of the three major trophies on show, having emerged from virtual bankruptcy four and a half years earlier, with the backdrop of a truly magnificent stadium, the chairman, the man who had made it all possible, was being heckled by people who would not even have been there but for his decision to go public.

This was my second AGM. My abiding memory of the first a year earlier was a shareholder near the front standing up, pointing aggressively, accusing Fergus McCann and shouting, 'McCann, you've done nothing for this club!' I was utterly incredulous. Perhaps the most significant thing of all that Fergus McCann had done was to permit that person to own shares and be at the meeting. But it was an incredible demonstration again of the uniqueness of Celtic.

I had to make a presentation to the AGM in September 1998 and, having watched Fergus enter into some kind of debate from time to time with the heckling shareholders ahead of my spot on the agenda, I decided that I would present my report as clearly as I could without faltering or hesitating, regardless of any attempts to heckle. That policy worked. I received an excellent hearing and throughout the bulk of my report relating to first-team matters there was not a sound from the audience. I should have stopped when I completed my report on first-team matters, because when I went on to youth development and sports science the rabble-rousers lost interest. It was significant, however, that during my entire report about first-team affairs you could almost have heard a pin drop.

I don't think this was what certain sections of the media expected. Overall it meant that the AGM passed relatively quietly, and certainly much more quietly than the pessimists had predicted. Why? I like to think that the vast majority of the shareholders are sensible and open-minded and are not driven by different agendas. They were prepared to listen to what was being said from the platform and I think they knew the information they were receiving was accurate and reflected a very healthy state of affairs within the club. The reaction I received from individual shareholders after the AGM was entirely positive and, indeed, heartening.

But there was a lot of water to flow under the bridge in the meantime. First, Jozef had confirmed that he would like to pursue interest in bringing Vidar Riseth from Lask Linz in Austria to the club. He had been considered carefully along with another midfield player but won the nod because he offered a degree of versatility which the other player did not – being able to provide effective cover at centre-back, for instance. Jozef had made the point on more than one occasion that he was a little concerned about the fact that most of our players were specialists in specific positions, with only Tommy Boyd in defence and Simon Donnelly and Darren Jackson in the middle to front area providing positional options. He believed that another couple of players who were similarly versatile would be important additions to the squad and Riseth fitted the bill particularly well in this respect, quite apart from the fact that he was an excellent player.

It had been established that Lask Linz had appointed agents in London to negotiate any transfer of the player, who had made it clear that he wanted to leave. I made contact with these agents and in a fairly short space of time agreed a satisfactory price to bring the player to the club. Once that was done, I was asked to send a fax direct to the club for the attention of their general manager, Max Hagmayr, outlining the details of our offer on the understanding that I would receive a fax by return accepting the offer.

This all happened on the morning of Friday, 19 September. That evening Riseth was supposed to play for his club in a league match but I had indicated to the agents that if agreement were reached I would prefer him not to play but instead to travel to London to meet me to discuss personal terms. I was told that the club officials were concerned about how they would explain to their supporters the absence of Riseth at short notice without any transfer being announced. I made it clear to the agents that this was a matter for Lask Linz. All I was asking was that he be withdrawn from the team that evening and given permission to travel to London. That is indeed what happened, although I believe that Lask Linz advised the press that he was unable to play because of a virus. That had nothing to do with me.

In any event, I travelled to London and spent Saturday negotiating and agreeing personal terms with Vidar. He explained to me at that meeting that the timing of the move was something of an embarrassment to him because friends had travelled from Norway for the weekend to watch him play on the Friday evening and then spend the weekend with him and his girlfriend. However, he had explained the position and they seemed to be totally supportive.

Vidar remained in London with his agents as I travelled back to Glasgow on the Saturday night. The agreement was that he would come to Glasgow for his medical on Monday morning with a view to signing on the terms agreed late on Monday afternoon.

The media had picked up on our interest from the Austrian end over the weekend and accordingly huge attempts were made by the press to contact Vidar to obtain confirmation of the position. At this time there was no attempt made to contact the club for confirmation since it had been clearly established that we would not comment on deals until they were complete.

I received a call from Vidar's agent on the Sunday evening to tell me about the relentless attempts by the press to reach Vidar in Austria. Apparently Vidar's girlfriend had taken one call and in a spirit of mischief had indicated that Vidar was there suffering from flu when the press were suggesting that he was in Glasgow in negotiations to come to Celtic. At one point Vidar's girlfriend had put his friend on the line as confirmation that Vidar was still in Austria. I was assured that this was all done in a spirit of fun but I realised instantly the potential rebound effect, particularly on Vidar, of such activity. I did say to Vidar's agent that I wished she had not done that because there were likely to be repercussions for the player when it was eventually established that he had travelled to Britain.

After completing his medical satisfactorily, Vidar duly signed late on Monday afternoon and a statement was issued to the press to the effect that he had signed and would meet the media the following day, Tuesday. Sure enough, having been misled from Austria without the knowledge of Vidar or Celtic, some sections of the press had a field day. They were clearly very upset at the fact that they had been deflected from the scent of the deal, so the story became all about the deception relating to the transfer. 'Jock Brown told us to lie!' said the *Daily Record*, which went on to purport to quote Max Hagmayr. It really represented a very interesting slant on how the media were dealing with matters. The story was not about Celtic's new signing, Vidar Riseth. It was all about the fact that the newspaper was indignant that it had been in some way duped about the details of the deal. How dare anyone not give them total co-operation and keep them fully abreast of the facts?

As is normal in the blame culture in which we all now exist, someone had to carry the can, and there was no one better than the man they had been attacking relentlessly for months, principally through their reporter Ewing Grahame.

Ewing Grahame is a man for whom I acted as solicitor some years ago. Perpetual attacks by him on me had obviously come to embarrass many of his colleagues and lots of members of the public, who continually asked me what I had done to him to generate such venom. I was eventually told by another member of the press that Ewing Grahame was claiming that I had botched up his divorce action. He was paying too much aliment, and it was my fault. This information was apparently given in answer to a question asking him why he constantly attacked me in such a vicious fashion.

Now I certainly acted for him in his divorce action, although I do not recall specific details about the case. However, I do not recollect at any time him expressing dissatisfaction with the service he received, nor did anything happen in the whole process which was in any way out of the ordinary. What I do recall, however, is receiving a telephone call from him at home one Sunday afternoon when he worked for *The Sun*, the *Daily Record*'s great rival. This was at a time when I was in a position to consider myself his solicitor and *after* my involvement, to the best of my recollection, in his divorce case. He asked me if I could give him some background on the legalities relating to the Duncan Ferguson case. You may recall that Duncan Ferguson was ordered off in a match for Rangers against Raith Rovers for an alleged headbutt and the matter came to the attention of not only the Scottish Football Association but also the Procurator Fiscal.

Ewing appeared to have no grasp whatsoever of what was involved in SFA regulations or in potential Crown proceedings. In fairness, he made no pretence at having such knowledge. He was asking me to mark his card so that he could write an authoritative piece. I duly did so, being as helpful as I possibly could and outlining to him all the ramifications of the procedures which could be involved. At no time was I being interviewed or providing information to be quoted. I was simply, as his solicitor, giving him some guidance on the matter so that he could write with some authority and accuracy. In the course of that discussion I expressed the view that I thought the SFA should wait until any criminal proceedings had been concluded before pursuing their own disciplinary procedures. I do recall saying that the SFA were off their heads to consider dealing with the matter in advance of the Crown.

Ewing thanked me profusely for all my assistance and I reverted to my normal Sunday afternoon pursuits of relaxing and reading the papers without giving the matter another thought.

The next morning I was driving to work when my brother Craig called me on my mobile telephone.

'What in the world are you up to?' he said. 'Have you seen *The Sun*?'

I told him I had no idea what he was talking about and he explained that *The Sun*'s inside back two pages contained a heading reading 'The SFA Are Off Their Heads'. It was then bylined 'by Jock Brown', with my photograph featured prominently, and branded 'exclusive'.

I was furious. It looked for all the world as if I had been party to a paid article for *The Sun* in which my byline would be used. Nothing could have been further from the truth. I considered the matter carefully with my legal colleagues and decided to send a fax to Ewing Grahame at *The Sun* which read, 'Please do not call me ever again.' Whether that fax reached him direct or arrived at the sports desk and was handed round all his colleagues before reaching him I will never know. I suspect, however, that it caused him some embarrassment and perhaps had some effect on the manner in which he treated me during my time at Celtic. That certainly rings more true to me than any suggestion of me botching his divorce action.

What concerns me more is that if several people had been able to tell me of his claims about his divorce action, then surely the hierarchy at the *Daily Record* should have been aware of that and should then have taken steps to ensure that any personal grudge he had, predating my time at Celtic, should not be allowed to influence his writing.

For me, the allegation that I had told someone to lie was the last straw. That is, for a lawyer, even worse than being accused of lying. It goes to the heart of my professional standing and had to become the subject of legal action. A writ was served on the newspaper immediately. This was done with the knowledge and blessing of the directors of Celtic. It resulted in a deluge of mail and messages to me congratulating me on starting legal proceedings and wishing me well. It really was staggering, the manner in which the public responded to the news that I had started legal action. It was also very encouraging.

I have never spoken to Max Hagmayr in my life. I sent a fax to Lask Linz for his attention but the response came from the president of the club, confirming the deal.

Doubts appeared to reach the *Daily Record* office about the accuracy of the 'told us to lie' story because the following day they produced another article quoting Vidar's agent as saying that my communication to this effect had been with him. So, in order to correct one possible wrong, in their eyes, they perpetrated another, because I had not been party to any such conversation with the agent either.

Whatever the outcome of the case, I most certainly did not tell anyone to lie, nor was I party to any kind of deception. All I did was conduct the transfer privately and confidentially until it was able to be announced. It really grieved me that the distortion of these events detracted from the positive impact of Vidar Riseth's arrival at the club.

With Vidar on board and Mark Viduka hopefully in the offing, Jozef Venglos was in the process of identifying two additional players he wanted to strengthen the squad. By this time his prediction about the difficulty with World Cup players had been proved correct in no uncertain terms. Morten Wieghorst was already a long-term casualty. Marc Rieper was clearly struggling and eventually had to have an operation which kept him out for a long time. Jackie McNamara struggled at the start of the season to overcome a knee problem which eventually required surgery and took him out of action. Craig Burley was suffering with a niggling groin injury which also necessitated a long-term absence in order to effect recuperation. So we lost the Players' Player of the Year for last season, Jackie McNamara, and the Football Writers' Player of the Year, Craig Burley, for lengthy periods. Simon Donnelly also missed many matches through injury as did Jonathan Gould and Darren Jackson. Only the apparently indestructible Tom Boyd and Henrik Larsson, together with Paul Lambert and the lightly used Tosh McKinlay, appeared to escape some kind of repercussion from the international matches in the summer.

Add to that the continuing long-term injury problems affecting Tommy Johnson and some intermittent problems for Alan Stubbs and Enrico Annoni, and you can see the extent to which the squad was decimated from time to time. Matches were drawn which really ought to have been won and some which should have been drawn were lost.

The first of the two new players identified by Jozef was Lubomir

Moravcik. In spite of having reasonable knowledge of foreign players dating back to my commentating days, I had no knowledge whatsoever of Moravcik, but Jozef told me that he was an immensely skilful player who would add a new dimension to our attacking play. However, he was very reluctant indeed to push his name because he was also Slovakian and he knew the kind of reaction he could expect from the media if he brought in one of his countrymen.

He explained that Moravcik had spent eight years in France with St Etienne and Bastia, having played under Jozef in the World Cup finals in Italy in 1990. Since that time he had moved to the German Bundesliga to play for Duisburg but he was not happy there because he was being used in a defensive midfield position when his principal attributes were creative. He had moved to Germany under the Bosman ruling.

Jozef further explained that Moravcik had played alongside Karel Poborsky and Patrik Berger in the Czech international team and was undoubtedly of the same quality. Since both these players had made an impact in the English Premiership with Manchester United and Liverpool respectively, it was clear that Moravcik was of a standard which justified interest from Celtic. However, Jozef remained very reserved about pushing Moravcik because he had now turned 33 and could not be deemed a long-term bet, although his build and fitness level were such that he should be able to play for two or three more seasons at the top level.

I indicated to the head coach that the only test which mattered initially was whether he was good enough to improve our squad. His nationality did not matter and we should not be deflected from pursuing interest in him simply because of the potential media reaction. Jozef was persuaded, subject to another look at the player in action to make sure that he had retained his fitness and his enthusiasm for the game. We arranged to travel to Bratislava to watch Slovakia play Portugal in a European Championship qualifier. Lubo was the captain of Slovakia.

In the match Slovakia were completely overrun by an outstanding Portuguese team, but every time Lubo went near the ball his quality was obvious. He is perhaps the most two-footed player I have ever seen and for a little man he was very good in the air. It was obvious that he was still very fit and he showed lots of enthusiasm.

More importantly, Jozef was satisfied about the player's technical ability and fitness although still very reserved about the impact the transfer would make in Glasgow if and when Lubo arrived. Once again, I was adamant that we should do the right thing by Celtic, regardless of potential reaction. Jozef was convinced. Accordingly, we opened negotiations with Duisburg and when Lubo heard of our interest he could not wait to get to Glasgow. Since he had not cost Duisburg anything and we were prepared to pay a transfer fee, albeit a modest one by modern standards, it became possible to agree a deal with the German club and thereafter with Lubo's agent on his personal terms.

When Lubo arrived in Glasgow the reaction was just as we had anticipated. It appeared as though no one within the football media had any idea about him. He was portrayed as 'Jozef's boy' and, frankly, his arrival was ridiculed in many quarters, largely because there was no huge transfer fee involved.

It told you a great deal about the media in Glasgow. Colin Hendry was born in exactly the same year as Lubomir Moravcik. He has approximately half the number of international caps held by Lubo and he was reported to have cost in excess of £4 million. His arrival in Glasgow was heralded as a major coup for Rangers and he effectively arrived to a fanfare of trumpets. In contrast, Lubo arrived to a host of criticism and ridicule: penny-pinching Celtic take the cheap route by bringing in an ageing ally of the head coach. Everything about his arrival appeared to be entirely negative.

That was until he played! He left the field in his debut against Dundee at Celtic Park to a standing ovation and entered Scottish football folklore when he scored the opening two goals in the 5–1 victory against Rangers in November. I was utterly delighted for Jozef Venglos.

Another feature was significant about that trip to Bratislava. The reaction to Jozef Venglos in his homeland had to be seen to be believed. I don't think I have ever seen one man shake so many hands in such a short time as Jozef did on his return to his native country. Not only the Slovakians bowed to him. When the Portuguese delegation arrived for the match, they too fell on his neck, demonstrating obvious respect and admiration. That reflected his time as coach at Sporting Lisbon.

Jozef's gentlemanly charm was conveyed in English, in Slovakian, of course, and in Portuguese. There were also people there from Poland and he spoke to them in their own language. The following morning, as we waited in Prague for a flight, he was approached by the Russian referee and his assistants who had been involved in a match in Prague the previous night. He conversed with them in Russian. To think that he has been subjected to criticism over his command of the English language by some journalists who are incapable of speaking their own mother tongue properly really makes my blood boil. I did my media case even more harm at one press conference when the question of his command of English was raised and I suggested that if they found any difficulty in communicating with him in English they could try one of the seven other languages he spoke fluently. I think the word was 'insular'.

Jozef Venglos is a world-renowned and world-respected figure. Paul Lambert found that out when he travelled with Jozef to take part in a celebration match for the Turkish Football Federation in Istanbul against a World XI coached by Jozef. The manner in which he was greeted by great football names like Dunga and George Weah must have spoken volumes. The fact that he was even invited to take charge of such a World XI, as he was again in Rome in December, speaks volumes too. One of the greatest benefits of my time at Celtic was the fact that I was privileged to have had the opportunity of getting to know Jozef Venglos. I treasure his friendship.

If he has a weakness as a coach in Britain it stems from the fact that he perhaps gives players *too* much respect. British players are used to hard-nosed managers who impose heavy discipline, like Alex Ferguson. Jozef Venglos expects every player to *want* to live properly, eat properly and practise diligently in order to hone his skills and become a better player. He does not believe that top-class players should have to be ordered about, curfewed on trips or told not to drink alcohol, eat the wrong things or miss out on sleep.

It seems to me that many British players are comfortable when they are subjected to very strict rules and disciplinary sanctions when the rules are broken. That is a cause for astonishment to an educated, intelligent man like Jozef Venglos. Yet in his playing career he was a tigerish, tough midfield player who played for Czechoslovakia in their great days in the early '60s. Jozef played alongside men like Masopust, who shared the number six jersey with Jim Baxter for the Rest of the World against England in 1963.

One of the greatest sadnesses of my departure from Celtic was the fact that I could no longer be in day-to-day contact with such a great man as Jozef Venglos, who has broadened my education not only in football but in life.

Throughout October the Mark Viduka saga took a series of twists and turns. The goalposts constantly moved and the signals coming from Croatia were consistently mixed. But I always had the feeling that he could become a Celtic player, despite suggesting to Jozef Venglos frequently the possibility of diverting our attention to an alternative striker. He insisted, though, that the prospects of bringing Viduka to the club must be explored to a conclusion, so we maintained our interest.

Alternative strikers were certainly considered. Another international centre-forward was investigated and became our second choice in the event that the Viduka deal broke down completely. One of our alternatives in the striking department was not John Spencer, despite another inflammatory story appearing in a tabloid newspaper. The suggestion was that I wanted to sign John Spencer but Jozef Venglos would not co-operate. It was the start of an attempt, no doubt, to drive a wedge between Jozef and me. The newspaper article quoted 'sources at Everton' as saying that I was very enthusiastic about the player.

What actually happened was that Jozef and I were travelling through Glasgow in my car when my mobile phone rang. An agent came on and asked if there was any possibility of there being interest in John Spencer from Everton. I responded politely and indicated that I would put the matter to our head coach, who had the say on such things, and revert. I did not indicate that Jozef was sitting beside me. I put down the phone and asked Jozef if he knew John Spencer. Naturally he did. I then asked him if he had any interest in pursuing his transfer to Celtic. Jozef responded that while Spencer was a very good player he did not believe he was the correct type of striker to link up with our existing players in that position, and accordingly he would not wish to pursue any interest.

Some two minutes after taking the original call I phoned the agent back and said that while we acknowledged that John Spencer was a very good player, he was not quite what Celtic were looking for at that particular time. I thanked the agent for the opportunity and asked him to wish Spencer well.

I have no doubt that the agent had indicated to Everton that he had contacts at Celtic and would try to find out if Celtic were interested. I presume that when he reported back he would have said that we had made very polite, complimentary noises about the player but that we were not proceeding at that time. How that became some kind of conflict between Jozef and me as to whether or not Spencer should be pursued could only be answered by the tabloid journalist concerned.

Yet virtually every day I was in discussion with one of the many agents involved to establish if and when Viduka could be the subject of successful negotiation. Eventually the breakthrough arrived when I received a telephone call while dining in a Glasgow hotel to the effect that the price had been agreed and the deal could be concluded. It meant another trip to Zagreb, which I have to confess had not become my favourite place.

This time I was met at the airport by one of the club's senior officials and taken to lunch with club officials at an excellent restaurant. It was clear that they were ready to do business. Eventually it was arranged that Mark Viduka would come to my hotel that evening to open up discussions with me and I spent a couple of hours with him. I found him to be very personable. We discussed mainly the footballing side of his transfer and arrangements for living and working in Glasgow rather than his personal terms, which were to be left for discussion with the agents he had finally appointed. Contact was made with his agents by telephone during our meeting and I was encouraged to believe that a deal could certainly be done. I was aware from our discussions of substantial difficulties experienced by Mark in Zagreb. But while I learned of many of the hurdles to be overcome, I was never left in any doubt that he was desperate to play for Celtic.

Until you have been involved in a transfer deal you have very little knowledge of what is actually involved and of the complexities which can prolong matters. Whereas Jonathan Gould took six and a half hours in all to sign, Paul Lambert took about three months and Mark Viduka roughly the same until his false start. The procedure is that the player to be purchased has to be identified by the head coach. Enquiries must be made with his existing club about his possible availability and then an agreement has to be reached on timing. A financial agreement must be drawn up between the two clubs agreeing the basis upon which the player can be transferred. Then the player must be given authority by the selling club to discuss personal terms with the purchasing club and that means a referral to agents. Agents do not work for nothing, so agreements need to be made with them. Selling clubs frequently appoint agents to act on their behalf, as Croatia Zagreb did, so there is another potential link in the chain. All these relationships have to operate smoothly in order for a transfer deal to be completed. If there is one link in the chain which breaks, the whole deal is in jeopardy. Time must be spent on each link.

That is why it still seems to me to be entirely inappropriate to say anything about transfer deals until they are complete. They could fall through at any moment and until the necessary signatures are on every contract there is no completed transaction. The ten agents involved in the Viduka deal guaranteed that a quick outcome was unlikely. There was also the possibility, although I cannot confirm this with direct knowledge, that there was discord among the officials of the selling club. They frequently have to argue out their position with regard to a potential sale, whether it be in respect of timing or of price, or even of the payment of instalments to give effect to settlement of the price. Not many clubs operate on a basis where one man can make all the decisions without conferring with his colleagues on the board of directors or with senior management. As you can imagine, you are dealing here with an emotive subject on which everyone has an opinion.

Further, once all of these competing interests have been satisfied, there is still the question of obtaining international clearance from one federation to enable a player to register with a club within another federation. If you add to all that the possible question of a work permit, then you have some idea of the overall complexity.

I was reporting constantly to Jozef Venglos on progress on the Viduka deal. We had to make repeated judgements as to whether or not to persist with our interest there or switch to our second choice. However, Viduka always remained the priority because it was believed that he would most satisfactorily fit in with our existing playing staff.

Simultaneously, Jozef wanted to strengthen the squad with another defender and the Swedish international Johan Mjällby was identified. Contact with his club, AIK Stockholm, was first made towards the end of October in the knowledge that the Swedish season ended early in November and AIK Stockholm were well in the running to win the championship. One of his attractions was his versatility in that he could play not only across the defence but also in a defensive midfield role. He was never intended to replace Paul Lambert, as some media experts speculated.

Once again the usual round of contacts was made and it became established that a transfer deal could be struck after the Swedish championship race had been concluded. Telephone calls were made and faxes exchanged in an attempt to reach an agreement, but it became apparent that if Johan Mjällby were to be signed, a personal visit to Stockholm was essential.

CHAPTER 20

At Odds with Lambert

The Paul Lambert saga took another twist late in October. Just as I was preparing to travel abroad, principally on the Viduka transfer, I was advised that Paul required to speak to me urgently. Because I was going to be absent from the office for a few days I spoke to him on the telephone, and during the course of the conversation it eventually became clear that he had written a book in which he had mentioned his perception of the difficulties about his arrival from Borussia Dortmund.

This was the first I had ever heard about him writing a book and I had substantial difficulty in obtaining from him a clear indication of the purpose of his call. Basically he felt it important to advise me in advance that he had mentioned his perception of my part in the alleged delay in his arrival at Celtic. He told me the book had been written 'in the summer', presumably prior to our lengthy discussion on the matter, and that the piece criticising me amounted to 'only about four lines, but you know what the newspapers will do with it when they get their hands on it'.

I asked him if he intended to have the book serialised and he said that the publishers had arranged this. It was a matter over which he had no control. He knew the newspapers would make a big thing out of his comments about me in relation to the transfer and thought it important to tell me in advance. The implication was that what was appearing did not reflect accurately his current feelings on the matter but clearly he felt that what was about to appear was outwith his control.

I suggested to Paul that in the event that the words did not represent accurately his current feelings, he would surely have had the chance to amend what had been said, but he explained that this was impossible. He also explained that he had no control at all over the way in which the newspaper would conduct the serialisation. Having had some experience as a lawyer of acting for people with material to publish, I was aware of the control elements which an author could exercise and I suggested to him that there would be no difficulty in him protecting himself by means of inserting appropriate clauses in the contract with the publisher. 'I don't know anything about that,' he said. I have no doubt he was telling the truth.

However, he omitted to tell me about the timing of the publishing of the book or, more importantly, the timing of the serialisation. There was no need whatsoever for me to ask him which newspaper would carry the serialisation because I had no basis for believing he was capable of the kind of sensitivity required to avoid selling the material to the publication which had caused the greatest offence to all his team-mates, the *Daily Record*.

I thanked him for his courtesy in alerting me to the situation in advance and set off about my business. It was only the following day when I was abroad that Peter McLean advised me that there had been a great panic over Paul Lambert's book since he wanted to know if the club shop would stock it despite his criticism of me. It had also become apparent that serialisation was beginning two days later, on the Saturday Celtic were scheduled to play Aberdeen at home.

Before a decision is taken on any book being sold in the club superstore there is obviously a requirement for it to be read by club officials, and that process would normally take two or three weeks at least. Paul gave the club about twenty-four hours. I was asked at long range what my attitude would be to the club stocking the book, and I indicated instantly that I would offer no objection on the basis of criticism of me which appeared in the publication and the decision could be taken by the appropriate club officials without further reference to me. I was asked if I wanted the material relating to me faxed to me for examination but I declined. I was told that 'it wasn't too bad'.

Frankly, I had much more pressing matters on my mind than the manner in which Paul Lambert sought to market his book and I knew perfectly well what was coming. Sure enough, when I landed at Heathrow Airport on the Saturday, I found myself sitting in the departure lounge for the shuttle to Glasgow opposite someone reading the *Daily Record* and pointing the back page at me. It carried the huge heading 'Why I Can't Stand Jock'. I have to confess that I managed a smile. The irony was that the material appearing beneath it did not justify the heading at all. Indeed, if you read the relevant passages in the book you will not find any justification for such a heading.

What made me angry, however, was the fact that Paul had allowed a hugely negative story to appear about Celtic on the morning of a crucial league match. For me, that is unforgivable. I also knew there was an issue for the club to handle arising from this material. It is clearly stated in players' contracts, including Paul's, that they cannot publicly voice criticism against the club or any of its representatives, so there was a clear breach of contract. Further, for him to take money from the newspaper which had been banned by all the players following the outrageous telephone message to Darren Jackson in Zagreb showed a complete disregard for the sensitivities of his team-mates.

In a way, Paul certainly has a great deal to thank me for in terms of cash generated by his book. Just about the only matter which anyone can recall about the publication of his life story appears to be his criticism of me. That very criticism would have made the *Daily Record* dig deep into their pockets to have the opportunity of creating such a headline in the safe and certain knowledge that there would be no complaint from the author of the book.

The matter was obviously discussed internally with Paul over the next few days. He was at great pains to tell me that while people frequently asked him how he felt about me, he was always playing the situation down. 'People think I hate you, but I don't hate you,' he told me. On that basis it saddened me to discover that he was at the same time confirming behind my back that he did hate me, all of which is a matter of supreme indifference in itself but doesn't say a great deal for Paul.

What became clear in discussing the matter with Paul and his agent, Gordon Smith, was that he had taken no advice at all in advance of the book being published. He expressed himself as unhappy that the book had been sold to the *Daily Record* and claimed he had had no control over that, or over the manner in which the paper used the material and prepared headings. When I put to him that there was nothing unusual about an author reaching an agreement with the publishers about which newspapers may be involved in the serialisation, about approving the edited version for serialisation, and about headings used in the material and about the timing for the use of the material so as not to derail the club's preparation for a match, he expressed total ignorance. I have no reason to disbelieve him.

In any event, the book was duly sold in the club shop. Paul appeared for a signing session which, sadly, didn't take him long and he eventually reached agreement with the club on an anodyne statement which was issued to the media in order to mitigate the effects of his breach of contract.

The whole affair saddened me. I found Paul an immensely likeable man in most respects, although remarkably opinionated and stubborn. I really believe he is a top-class player, although, as I have already indicated, I feel he actually sells himself a little short, considering the ability at his disposal. His dedication to his family must be respected and admired but it would be even more admirable if he extended a little more consideration to other people's families. In fairness, he did exchange suitable pleasantries with me after hearing the news of my departure. I suspect his first thought was that it had nothing to do with him. In that he would be right.

I did not get back in time to see the match against Aberdeen, which was won by virtue of two goals from Simon Donnelly. By this time we were locked in the struggle to progress in Europe against FC Zurich. It would really be a tragedy for us to go out against opposition of that moderate quality but the fates did militate against us in both legs.

At Celtic Park a good first-half performance had us leading by a goal to nil approaching half-time when a mix-up between Jonathan Gould and Stephane Mahe resulted in Tom Boyd having to make a save with his hands inside the penalty box. This resulted in a penalty kick, which was missed, but, more significantly, a red card for the skipper. The second half was played very sensibly with ten men against eleven, Celtic seeking to ensure a clean sheet to take a lead to Zurich, but a freak goal near the end gave the Swiss a vital away goal.

The second leg was obviously extremely difficult but was made even more so by the fact that ten first-team players could not be considered for selection. Eight were injured and two key men, Tom Boyd and Craig Burley, were suspended. The handicap was too great to overcome. While we were ridiculed in many sections of the media for going out to a less-than-top-quality opponent, too little regard, in my opinion, was paid to fates which had conspired against us. A 4–2 defeat put us out of Europe and certainly reflected a major disappointment for the season.

In that match in Zurich, Jonathan Gould's run of 70 consecutive matches came to an end when he had to come off injured in the second half, although I must confess to having taken substantial pleasure from the fact that Stewart Kerr was able to come on as substitute. Having made such an auspicious start to his Celtic first-team career, Stewart had been extremely unlucky with injury and had not featured at all during Wim Jansen's season in charge. By the time he was fully fit he was frustrated by the fact that Jonathan Gould's excellent form prevented him from experiencing first-team football, and I had agreed a deal with him around August that detailed consideration of his position would be carried out at the end of September, regardless of our European status. The appropriate meeting was held immediately after we qualified by beating Vittoria Guimaraes to progress further in Europe, and an agreement was reached whereby Stewart would be allowed to leave if a satisfactory offer was received from another club, subject only to our requirements for European cover being met.

A couple of weeks later I spoke to Stewart to ask him if he had had any indication of interest from other clubs and within that conversation I asked him if it would be possible to settle him down by negotiating a new contract with him to remain with Celtic. He undertook to consider that and came back to me the following day to say he would be interested in considering an extended, improved contract because he really didn't want to leave Celtic but was concerned about his career generally and about doing the best he could for his family.

On that basis I was happy to obtain the approval of the directors to negotiate with him a new improved and extended contract to keep him at the club until 2003. The feeling is that this may turn out to be one of the best pieces of business I did for the club, because I share the professionals' view that young Stewart is a top-class keeper with a big future. He is almost seven years younger than Jonathan Gould, so I'm sure his time will come.

Other contract-management issues had become important since discussions had to be held with players going out of contract, such as Simon Donnelly, Phil O'Donnell, Tosh McKinlay, Brian McLaughlin, Morten Wieghorst and Mark Burchill. It also seemed important to me to consider further the year ahead, which is why the question of extending Henrik Larsson's contract was also raised with him in the early part of the season.

Malky Mackay was another player who would have been out of contract at the end of the season but I was very pleased for him that a transfer to Norwich City was able to be completed in September. This was a move which I think made sense for all parties concerned and it certainly ended a period of frustration for Malky following the difficulties of the previous season.

So there was still a lot of work to be done on all fronts, but for me time was rapidly running out.

CHAPTER 21

Time to Go

Celtic is, without question, a unique club. It generates so much passion and affection that frequently those who contribute so much negativity and trouble are people who initially cared deeply. There is one stark distinction between Celtic and Rangers which has intrigued me over the four decades in which I have been first an interested onlooker, then a direct participant. People who work at Rangers, whether as players, managers or coaches, are seldom heard offering criticism towards the current custodians of the club's fortunes. Quite the contrary afflicts Celtic.

The argument will be that Rangers have over that period treated their employees better than Celtic have theirs. That is apparently why you see very few signs of bitterness from ex-Rangers men whereas it appears to be the norm for ex-Celtic people. I am sorry, but I do not buy that. Obviously, I have no detailed knowledge of the manner in which both clubs have treated their employees over all that time, but I am sure it is much too simple to dismiss this issue with such an explanation.

I know of people who have had bad experiences at Rangers but will never denounce the club publicly. Yet when there are any issues involving Celtic in the public eye, you know there will be a queue of 'Celtic-minded' people ready to put the boot in and spread poison. It is frequently those who claim the 'Celtic-minded' status who are so vociferous in speaking up against the club. Surely if they cared so much about the well-being of the organisation, even if they had private concerns, they would keep their negativity to themselves. But within the football club we always knew what names to expect to be trotted out on a 'rent-a-quote' basis to cater to the media agenda.

We are talking here of a club which was on the brink of extinction as a major force early in 1994 and which is now, by any standards, totally revitalised in every aspect of a modern football club. Yet the critics carrying the 'Celtic-minded' badge cannot wait to respond to media requests to savage the club. If it wasn't so sad it would be laughable.

It seems to me that Rangers Football Club is perceived as more of an institution and, as such, commands respect from its supporters. Celtic, on the other hand, is much more of a family, and thus generates infinitely more emotion. Supporters, even those who are not share-holders, appear to feel as though they own a little bit of Celtic and everything that happens generates an emotional reaction. Emotions come in all sorts of forms, from love to hate, anger, indignation, joy and sorrow.

There appears to be much more of a siege mentality about Celtic, and I certainly subscribed to that during my time. It seems there is a great degree of trust on the part of Rangers supporters in those charged, from time to time, with the task of running their club. Celtic supporters, on the other hand, don't appear to show similar trust. Why else would Fergus McCann be subjected for so long to abuse? There may well be justification both historically and in the modern era for such a siege mentality but I am sure it is frequently anything but productive. Whether it will ever change is a moot point. It may be too deeply imbedded.

My principal offence was not to play the media game the way the media wanted. I knew there could only be one loser. But it was vital to be true to myself in accepting the brief I had been given from Celtic and in implementing it right down the line regardless of the effect on my personal position.

What were the crimes which justified a campaign described to me by many experienced observers as unprecedented in its relentlessness and viciousness? First, I took too long over the appointment of a head coach before Wim Jansen arrived. Well, he was appointed two weeks after I was appointed and many weeks after the search for both a head coach and a general manager had begun. Secondly, I misled the media over the Paolo Di Canio situation. Actually I didn't, because the circumstances changed so rapidly that I had to move with equal speed to make certain that Celtic's interests were served to the best possible effect.

Thirdly, I took too long to complete transfer deals. With nine new players costing more than £12 million brought to the club within the space of some five months on contracts which have generated no difficulties whatsoever – and if there is any understanding at all of what is involved in bringing in new players in the early part of a season, especially if they are coming from a foreign country – I plead not guilty.

Fourth, Wim Jansen could not work with me and because of me he left. In actual fact, Wim Jansen was leaving Celtic after one season no matter what happened. That is my clear belief. Besides, in the event that there is any lack of harmony between two employees in a club, surely it is only fair and reasonable to start from the position that there must be faults on both sides. I certainly accept that and would never claim to be blameless in relation to my failure to become bosom buddies with Wim. However, after more than thirty years of full-time employment without ever being conscious of inherent difficulties in getting on with colleagues, and remaining on excellent terms with most of my former colleagues, I prefer to take the view that my failure in this case was in relation to Wim Jansen specifically rather than the world generally. It has been well documented that Wim fell out with his president at Feyenoord, having also fallen out with the coach there at the time of his departure from that club.

Fifth, I took too long to appoint a replacement head coach after Wim's departure. How in the world can I accept blame for that in the circumstances already narrated and bearing in mind that I was an employee of the club and did not sit on the board?

Sixth, I took too long to bring in new players at the start of season 1998–99. I have already made it clear that I could only move on transfers when the head coach told me who he wanted and the board sanctioned the deal. Then we frequently had to deal with the vagaries of the international transfer business, as exemplified by Mark Viduka's transfer from Croatia Zagreb.

So the only accusation to which I would plead guilty is that I did not play the game with the media. Whether I would have played it any differently if left to my own devices remains a matter of privacy between the board of directors and me. My conscience is clear on one essential point: at no stage during my time at Celtic did I ever put my own personal interests ahead of Celtic's.

I prefer to reflect on the fact that when I arrived at Celtic there were only two full-time coaches, no head coach and a heavily depleted playing squad. There was also the task of trying to prevent Rangers from achieving a record of ten championships in a row. I played my part in the arrival of Wim Jansen and Murdo MacLeod, completed nine inward transfers before Christmas, watched the Coca-Cola Cup being won and then embarked on the most trying and wearing policy of appeasement towards the head coach with only one end in mind, the winning of the championship, which was achieved.

Massive profits were generated from the recalcitrant stars Paolo Di

Canio and Jorge Cadete, who had made it clear they would never pull on the hoops again. There were no contractual misunderstandings or players with 'little problems'. Several players left the club to pursue careers elsewhere but we parted amicably. A top-class development coaching staff was recruited and the development programme for youngsters within the club has never been stronger. The sports science initiatives sought by Brian Scott have been implemented to ensure that Celtic remains at the forefront of fitness technology.

But I did not have media approval. That meant antagonism from the tabloid-reading supporters when every game was not won and vast sums of money were not spent on new players on a regular basis. I was portrayed as arrogant, over-confident, uncivil, rude and condescending. Further, I was supposed to be overbearing, I wanted to pick the team, I wouldn't entertain anyone who disagreed with me and I was contemptuous towards colleagues and members of the media. I was a monster, the Antichrist, a demon.

It is an incredible experience to be subjected to such vitriol over such an extended period, especially when you believe the attacks to be unwarranted. More importantly, directors, colleagues, friends and associates were appalled by it all and supremely supportive. But the time I had first mentioned to Fergus McCann in September had come. I had become anathema in the eyes of the Celtic supporters, or 'customers'. A relentless portrayal of fiction had taken on the mantle of reality. I had to be sacrificed.

The reference to 'customer' is significant in that I attended a function at which George Galloway MP castigated Fergus McCann for referring to Celtic supporters as 'customers'. I felt compelled to challenge Mr Galloway privately and explained to him that referring to Celtic supporters as customers meant that they were being treated in appropriate fashion for people who were so important. Part of the historical problem at Celtic was, in my opinion, the fact that the support of so many people was taken for granted, No matter how badly they were treated they would always come back because of their love for the club and their wish to support it. Fergus McCann introduced the notion that supporters should be treated as customers. Customers must be wooed and attended to properly to ensure that they provide repeat business not only because of their love for the club but also because of the good treatment they receive.

Mr Galloway paid lip service to understanding this but his prejudice was apparent. He was one of the 'Celtic-minded' people who was against so much that was happening at Celtic. He made it clear to

Kirsty Wark shortly after my departure how low his opinion of me was. Yet he had only spoken to me once at that function and had no direct knowledge of any work which I was doing within the club. So much for being an evidence man. As he is so frequently criticised in the press himself, I was surprised at his lack of perspicacity and research.

The essential trip to Sweden had just been carried out. There had been lengthy discussions about the acquisition of Johan Mjällby from AIK Stockholm and I had also had the opportunity of dining with Claes Elefalk, the IMG representative who was acting as agent for Mark Viduka. Progress was made on both counts and, happily, both eventually became Celtic players, but I knew before setting off for Stockholm that the sands of time were running out for me. The venom was still apparent every time my name was mentioned in certain sections of the media.

It had become impossible for me to carry out all the tasks set out for me in my job description. In particular, I was no longer able to speak out in the media on football matters on behalf of the club without the effect being negative on the club. Similarly, it had become impossible to continue as a liaison between the club and the supporters because of the vote of no confidence.

I could sense within the stadium the unease and the sympathy felt by so many of my colleagues for the predicament in which I found myself. It was seldom, if ever, a topic for discussion but people within the organisation clearly realised what had happened. I have no doubt they believed the treatment of me was unfair, but they appreciated the impotence of all of us to turn things around.

During Wim Jansen's time at the club, it was my duty to attend all pre-match press conferences with him. He was generally out of the press room five minutes after the start, having provided the press with his squad for the match and an injury list to explain absentees. I was then left to deal with all the other questions, which normally lasted a very long time.

When Jozef Venglos arrived, a decision was taken that I should not accompany him to press conferences because of the potentially negative outcome which would result. It was recognised that virtually anything I said at such a press conference would result in negative coverage for the club and another pasting for me. I never felt comfortable about that because, regardless of the effect on me personally, I felt it was very important to carry out my duties as they had been set out, especially if I could be helpful to Jozef, who was initially totally bewildered by the manner in which the press went about their business. He quickly realised that he could attend a press conference for an hour and a half which appeared to have gone well until one question at the end generated a battery of negative headlines the following day, with the bulk of the material already provided in a positive fashion ignored.

The treatment Jozef received from sections of the media in the first half of the season was, in my opinion, nothing short of disgraceful. He was portrayed as some kind of shambling, indecisive illiterate, with constant references to his alleged difficulties with the English language. In truth, he is a supremely intelligent, well-educated man whose command of English is infinitely better than many of those who saw fit to criticise. It goes without saying that his command of the other seven languages at his fingertips was one hundred per cent better than that of most of his critics!

Jozef had another problem, I suspect, with many sections of the press. He clearly got on well with me and there was never any prospect of him portraying any discord within the camp. After my departure, nothing gave me greater pleasure – especially as it came at the point when sections of the tabloid press were winding up, it appeared to me, against him, to go for the kill – than seeing him orchestrate the biggest victory over Rangers in 32 years, inspired on the pitch by the little genius called Moravcik whose arrival at the club for such a modest transfer fee had generated so much ridicule.

But journalists had stopped calling me to check on things and to ask for responses to their endless speculation about players coming and going. More importantly, the club was not winning enough matches and the natives were becoming increasingly restless. Commercial business was slowing up and something had to happen which would be perceived as massively positive by the Celtic support. That something was my departure.

I returned from Stockholm on Friday, 6 November, to a goalkeeping injury crisis and a lengthy debriefing with Fergus McCann. It was time for me to go. It broke my heart to acknowledge this, but the time had come. The principle of departure was established that Friday evening with Fergus and the mechanics were left to be resolved on Saturday morning. In between, it was vital to me that I spent time with Jozef Venglos. I spent the remainder of the evening at his home, discussing and clarifying the overall situation. I could not have been in better company for the purpose.

The next morning the details were clarified and arrangements made for me to co-operate in the fullest possible way with a smooth handover of ongoing business over the next couple of weeks. After the news had been released, I made my way out of Celtic Park just before the home match against Dundee, which was won by six goals to one – allegedly, in some quarters, a victory inspired by my departure!

While the news of my leaving Celtic generated delirium among many of the supporters who had faithfully believed so much of the media propaganda and a degree of hysteria from the media generally, the reaction I received personally was totally remarkable. I received a host of supportive telephone calls from players and staff at the club, prominent people in the game both north and south of the border and even some members of the media. I also received an avalanche of letters, including two magnificent ones from the plc directors Brian Quinn and Sir Patrick Sheehy.

I also received letters from people I had never heard of but who had obviously been interested onlookers as the saga of my time at Celtic unfolded. This one was indicative of the type of correspondence I received:

Dear Jock

I wish to express my sadness over your departure from Celtic last weekend.

My feelings are that, in the light of circumstances, what has happened was perhaps inevitable, but my sadness is more to do with the way you have been treated since the beginning, not only by the media, but especially by the many charlatans and imposters who represent themselves as being 'Celtic-minded'.

After forty years of following the club it has been a humbling experience to realise that the bigots in the so-called Celtic Family are not confined to those who sing sectarian and political songs but clearly include a large group of better-off fans whose noses were put out of joint at your appointment. What has proved even more disturbing has been the spectacle of so many True Celts rushing to the press to sell their own jaundiced and bitter versions of their stories with little regard to the damage they were doing to the club and the morale of the support in general.

As you will no doubt have noted, the fact that many of these characters had no real gripe with the way they were treated, or indeed lost cases which they chose to bring to court, was rarely reported in any depth at all. I also noted how often you defended these people in the press when they were your colleagues even

185

though it must have been very difficult knowing everything you knew about them and their behaviour.

On TV last Sunday, Billy McNeill said that he had regarded your appointment as a good move by the club, and that your many qualities were in fact exactly what Celtic required. Perhaps if he had made such statements sixteen months ago then those who were ready to label you as 'not Celtic-minded' would have been deflected by the support of such an ikon (sic) for your appointment.

Thank you for your efforts on our behalf, and for your contribution to the championship win last season. About a year ago you wrote in the *View* about attending the Requiem Mass for the deceased members of the Supporters' Association in St Mary's. Your appreciation of that single event said more about your right to be in the job than anything said by your critics.

Yours sincerely

I also received innumerable requests both orally and in writing to record my time at the club in this book.

My last major public engagement as General Manager, Football, at Celtic was the following day, Sunday, when I held a press conference at Celtic Park which lasted the bulk of the afternoon. The attendance at the press conference was overwhelming. Radio broadcasts were being relayed live from Celtic Park, although I had requested no live coverage of the conference itself.

'Did you jump or were you pushed?'

I expected little else from Davie Provan, whose antipathy and venom had been apparent at virtually every interview over many months, making me wonder about the wisdom of the endless hours in an earlier life spent with him trying to help him become a television broadcaster, and insisting on him being used by BSkyB as a football reporter on Scottish matches despite being told from London 'On your head be it'.

After the Davie Provan opener, the questions centred on who I was seeking to blame for my departure and what mistakes I had made during my time. It was clear in my mind that I would be apportioning blame nowhere and would accept total responsibility for my situation. We are undoubtedly in a blame culture. This is apparent everywhere around us. It is almost always the first reaction to any development in the public eye. Whose head must roll? Whose fault was it? Who is to blame?

I sought then and seek now to blame no one. I was conscious when I accepted the post at Celtic that it would inevitably be short term. The job description and job specification ensured that. There was no way in the world the media would accept having to deal with someone who was not picking the team and who was implementing a board policy (with which I agreed) to take the running of the football club into a new and progressive stage under a new structure. Unless this involved feeding the media in appropriate ways at appropriate times in a period of unqualified success for the team on the pitch, someone would have to carry the can – and it was sure to be the general manager.

So I entered this exciting phase of my life with my eyes wide open. I was well aware of the workings of the media, although I have to confess to underestimating the intensity of the interest in Celtic and the viciousness and venom with which certain elements of the media went about their campaign to attack me. In these circumstances, how could I deflect blame to anyone?

Of course, I made mistakes, many of which never reached the public's attention. The major one to which I admitted at the press conference was misjudging the handling of the media. I certainly did, because while I knew broadly the way in which they worked, I did not fully appreciate the absence, in some quarters, of industry, balance and fairness. I certainly failed on a number of occasions to conceal my frustration and disappointment with some members of the media. When that happens, you are a guaranteed loser.

After spending the afternoon with newspaper, radio and television journalists, attempting to get everything completed in one fell swoop, I was able to withdraw to the splendid company of Jozef Venglos and Eric Black. I did not listen to a radio programme, watch a television programme, or read a line of the press covering my departure. I am aware that they had a field day but suddenly and quickly it was all over. It was a welcome return to a degree of anonymity. The impact of the sacrifice was what was expected and the exercise was justified.

It was fascinating, too, to receive offers from tabloid newspapers for my 'exclusive story'. Publications which had previously 'slaughtered' me now wanted to give me money!

But it was interesting to be told of what the media had expected from me at that press conference. Apparently I was to spend the time justifying myself and blaming other people for my departure. I would have a blast at various people. No doubt they hoped that I would attack the club and, even better, Fergus McCann. But there was no possibility of that. I have nothing but the warmest of feelings for Celtic Football Club and for those who made my time there so unforgettable.

It is such a well-run club and there are so many excellent people employed there. I feel privileged to have met so many outstanding people within so many different facets of the organisation, from commercial, catering and publishing to ticket sales, secretariat and administration. It really was a joy to walk past the front-door reception to work every day. With the exception of the chasm between Messrs Jansen and MacLeod and the development staff, including me, the atmosphere internally was always excellent and most problems were generated externally by people with many different agendas.

The club will flourish, let there be no doubt about that. Fergus McCann was absolutely the right man, perhaps the only man, to lead Celtic out of the abyss in March 1994. But I think a different style of leadership may now be required to take the club on an expansionist future. My own view is that the miracles of the past five years have served to rescue the organisation but have only scratched the surface of the club's potential. The club makes a worldwide impact and generates ferocious loyalty which can and must now be harnessed to create an environment whereby the target which I expressed shortly after my arrival is achieved, namely that when the quarter-final draw is being made for the European Champions' Cup, seven other clubs are praying they don't draw Celtic.

People have asked me countless times if I regretted leaving my safe, comfortable professional life in the law and broadcasting to join Celtic. The answer is always the same – I do not regret going to Celtic for one second.

My departure from Celtic was unique in many ways. There was absolutely no aggravation or animosity. There wasn't a cross word. In a world where the normal situation is to clear your desk and leave instantly, I retained the freedom of Celtic Park to tidy up ongoing matters and to ensure a smooth transition.

Two days after my resignation, I attended a meeting with Fergus, Eric Riley, Jozef Venglos, Eric Black and Tom Boyd to discuss how the handover would be carried out and who would pick up the various aspects of my work. Players and other members of staff called in to see me in numbers on that Monday, so much so that I indicated to Fergus that I thought I should leave the building. Many of my colleagues didn't know exactly how to communicate with me in circumstances of such an amicable departure.

On that basis, it was agreed that I should spend the following day doing as much as I possibly could to prevent the need for me to come in on a daily basis afterwards. On that Tuesday, players came in and out of my office after training and one of them, a top international player certainly not renowned for being the emotional type, sat in my room for the best part of two hours. There was an air of amicable sadness which had to be brought to end by my departure from the building. My only regret is that circumstances were such that I could no longer play a hands-on part in what I am sure will be a triumphant journey into the future.

I wasn't the only departure from Celtic at that time. My secretary and personal assistant, Betty Pryde, went with me. We first met when I joined the Motherwell law firm Ballantyne and Copland in 1973, when she was the secretary to the senior partner. In 1987, when the senior partner retired, she became my secretary/personal assistant and has remained my right arm ever since, moving with me when I became a Sports Law Consultant at Harper Macleod in Glasgow and then to Celtic.

I had confided in her in September that my time at the club was running out. She said then that she would leave whenever I did, although she is very close to retirement. Sure enough, when the time for my resignation came and I contacted her at home she indicated immediately her intention to resign with me. I know that the club would have much preferred her to stay and I also knew with complete certainty that the players would be desperate for her to remain at the club because she had become such an ally to them. To their credit, Fergus McCann and Eric Riley tried very hard indeed on the Monday morning to persuade her to stay with the club notwithstanding my departure, but she was adamant that she could no longer continue if I were leaving.

For my own part, I would have been perfectly happy for her to stay since she was a huge loss to the club, a fact which was recognised by everyone inside Celtic Park. She had no job to go to and her retirement position was clearly going to be adversely affected as far as her pension was concerned. But nothing would shake her from her decision to leave, and her personal loyalty to me is something I will never forget. It also occurred to me in my low moments, when I wondered if I *had* become the ogre many sections of the media portrayed, that I couldn't be that bad if I still enjoyed the trust, friendship and support of a lady of this quality.

Lessons have undoubtedly been learned from my 510 days at Celtic Park, both by me and by the club. There is no doubt whatsoever in my mind that the structure set up by the board in the summer of 1997 is correct for modern times. However, a different approach to communicating with supporters needs to be adopted and, I am sure, is being adopted. The only way to communicate with supporters is through the media. Only the players and, to a large extent, the head coach, are exempt in that they can create a relationship with supporters simply by their performances on the field of play. Such a privilege is not extended to directors and management. Accordingly, if they fall foul of the media, the message to supporters is negative. Whether those in power like it or not, they have to form relationships with the media which give them an even chance of communicating actively and positively with the supporter base. Much more time must be allocated to this and much more care must be taken.

When I arrived in June 1997, the quest for the new head coach was at its height and one of the principal priorities communicated to me was confidentiality in respect of every move being made. There was, in all honesty, a degree of paranoia about this and I am certain it did not serve us well. While there was a degree of perverse satisfaction about producing first Wim Jansen then Jozef Venglos right out of the blue, it turned out to serve neither the club nor the new head coaches well. It was utterly amazing to see the status acquired in a short period of time by Gerard Houllier in the eyes of the Scottish media when they thought he would be the new head coach at Celtic, whereas the reaction to the real target, Jozef Venglos, was, frankly, appalling.

Clear lessons can be learned. Jozef Venglos would have been easier to package as an outstanding selection over a two- or three-week lead-in period than Houllier. Similarly, a player like Vidar Riseth would have had a much better reception had he been the subject of discussion in the press for some days before he arrived. The fear at Celtic was always that any deals in contemplation would break down before the ink was dry on the contract. The siege mentality was such that everyone at the club was aware of the fact that the club would be portrayed as 'bungling', or once again 'in turmoil', if a proposed deal did not come to fruition. The parading of Maurice Johnston in 1989 before he had signed, and then losing him to Rangers, continued to haunt those of us involved in recruiting players.

I undoubtedly carry blame for not influencing that state of affairs for the better. Having gone under siege myself so early in my time at Celtic, I was constantly determined to demonstrate that I was not seeking to look after my own interests, but only Celtic's. The error of judgement there was that had I looked after my own interests better, I would also have been looking after Celtic better.

While people were apparently always amazed at what they saw as remarkable strength in me as I withstood the media onslaught, perhaps they would also be amazed at me remaining so blinkered in my determination to justify trust from my employers that I did not make a major issue of trying to resolve my media predicament.

Overall, for me, it is sad that my time in a difficult job had to come to an end at a point where I was probably best able to cope with it.